BUSINESS ENVIRONMENT
AND BUSINESS ETHICS

Ballinger Series in

BUSINESS IN A GLOBAL ENVIRONMENT

S. Prakash Sethi, Series Editor

Center for Management
Baruch College
The City University of New York

BUSINESS ENVIRONMENT AND BUSINESS ETHICS
The Social, Moral, and Political Dimensions of Management

edited by

KAREN PAUL

BALLINGER PUBLISHING COMPANY
Cambridge, Massachusetts
A Subsidiary of Harper & Row, Publishers, Inc.

International Standard Book Number: 0-88730-204-1

Library of Congress Catalog Card Number: 87-3573

Printed in the United States of America

Library of Congress Cataloging-in-Publication Data

Business environment and business ethics.

(Ballinger series in business in a global environment)
Bibliography: p.
Includes index.
1. Business ethics. 2. Industry—Social aspects.
I. Paul, Karen. II. Series.
HF5387.B867 1987   174'.4   87-3573
ISBN 0-88730-204-1

Contents

List of Tables

Preface

Business schools are in a paradoxical position in relation to both the business and the academic communities. The critical role of business faculty is sometimes hard for the business community to understand and accept. As long as faculty concentrate on operational questions, their problem-defining role is somewhat more likely to be appreciated. But when the focus is on the rights and wrongs and shoulds and oughts of business, on moral responsibilities, on the economic, social, and ethical potential and shortcomings of business institutions, on the personal and increasingly the legal obligations of management, on the specific qualities associated with business leadership, the role of the business school becomes more complex and controversial.

The esteem with which the business school has been regarded in academe has been less than total. Business schools historically have had standards of research and scholarship rather more flexible than some other faculties, including the arts and sciences, which have generally provided the intellectual leadership of the modern university. The more traditional areas of the university have had a tendency to dismiss the business school on grounds of inadequate scholarship. Other arts and sciences faculty often distrust business institutions and business values, and so brand as lacking the business school intellectual interests. Some professional schools, most notably engineering, law, and medicine, have come to play a central role in the modern university. But these schools have a clear link to their constituencies, generally controlling entry into occupations. Even mediocre professional schools typically have a research-driven faculty (less so in law schools), but this is only recent in business schools. And, of course, in past decades the other professional schools have been able to attract more capable students than have business schools.

Hence the paradox—being of, but not completely so, both the business community and the academic community. This position makes it particularly important for the business school and its faculty to develop solid, theoretically well-grounded scholarship. In the past generation, business schools have gone a long way toward remedying past deficits. Theory development and empirical research are alive and well. This book documents this intellectual substance in the business-environment and business-ethics area.

Both operational questions and value questions are the object of scholarship in the business school, but the focus of this work is mainly on the value questions, specifically, how should business look at, understand, and become responsible to the surrounding society. "Business environment" is the term generally used to refer to the social, legal, and moral forces behind business institutions. "Business ethics" relates to the moral ramifications of decisionmaking both on the level of the individual manager and on the organizational or collective level. But operational questions are also involved, so that the significance of this topic is more than just philosophical. Managers need to know how to make decisions in the context of accepted ethical norms, how to establish structures and procedures that will reward that behavior sanctioned by the organization, and how to assess intelligently the social, political, and moral dimensions of the environment in which they operate. Certain organizational structures and processes, certain guidelines for managerial attitudes and actions, certain values will encourage effective managerial behavior and executive decisionmaking among those who are receptive to the idea of the social responsibility of business.

A final aim of this work is to record current developments in the business-ethics/business-environment field, the area covering the social, legal, and economic environment of business in the business curriculum. For nearly twenty years, the American Assembly of Collegiate Schools of Business has mandated this area as an essential component of business education. The ways in which business schools meet this expectation are varied, yet all revolve around certain basic themes and models identified here.

A group of dedicated individuals worked together to produce this collective summary of the field of business environment/business ethics. This community of scholars invested time, energy, and intellectual talent to compile a reference work of the past several decades in this field and to point toward likely future developments. Our respective institutions each backed us in our efforts, as did a generous grant by the General Electric Foundation and the support of the Governance Board of the Social Issues in Management Division of the Academy of Management.

Encouragement for this project came from a number of individuals within the fields of business environment and business ethics. Professors Edwin Epstein, Ballinger's Consulting Editor, and S. Prakash Sethi, Series Editor for the Series in Business in a Global Environment were especially supportive, as were Professors Walter Klein, William Frederick, and Gerald Cavanaugh. East Coast support of the project was provided by the College of Business at the Rochester Institute of Technology. On the West Coast and for the business-ethics portion of the project headed by Otto Bremer, the Vesper Society was most supportive.

Elaine Tandy did an extraordinary job of making sense of masses of bits and pieces of materials coming from a great diversity of sources in a wide variety of forms. Her skill at utilizing modern word-processing technology to the fullest while accommodating the disparate expectations of a group of academics deserves much credit. The continuing support and encouragement provided by Management Department Secretary Ellie Lavell merits a special thanks. Graduate Assistant Peter Maynard contributed to the project in its early days, while Graduate Assistant Robin Faillace helped enormously in its final days, showing great resourcefulness and creativity in tracking down elusive materials, and sometimes elusive people.

CHAPTER 1

Business Environment and Business Ethics in Management Thought

Karen Paul

A wide range of ethical expectations and social responsibilities are now incumbent upon today's managers and corporations. Managers are called upon to participate in revitalizing the economy and making it competitive in world markets. They are expected to find ways to restructure their organizations so that both productivity and the self-realization of employees are more fully achieved. The preparation of managers has become complex. The manager must be capable of understanding a variety of rapidly changing technologies, yet able to look beyond mere technical requirements and function effectively in the work organization and in society. Recent critiques of higher education such as *A Nation at Risk* (National Commission on Excellence in Education 1983) and *College: The Undergraduate Experience in America* (Boyer 1987) emphasize the importance of the educational mission to develop the capacity to understand and integrate new information coming from society, to deal with issues of values, and to act in an ethically aware fashion. In the business school, business environment and business ethics comprise the part of the curriculum where these competencies are developed most directly.

Just about twenty-five years, a generation of time, have passed since this area of the business curriculum began to be defined. A vast expansion in societal expectations of corporations and of managers occurred as a result of the social turmoil that swept through the United States beginning with the civil rights movement of the late 1950s and 1960s, continuing through the antiwar movement of the 1960s and 1970s, and culminating in the various revelations following the Watergate scandal of the early 1970s. The demands of consumers, of women, of environmentalists have impelled many of the changes in the corporate environment over this period. However, in recent years, issues regarding the basic integrity of the American economy have increased in importance. Questions about trade policy, productivity, and the structure of American industry have produced a new set of topics that are now central to the field of business environment.

A second influence shaping the field has come from several different sources in the external society. It is rather ironic that business circles proper have begun to show a keen interest in business ethics, while most business schools remain at a rather primitive stage of development with regard to these issues. Increasingly, corporations have evolved their own training programs in this area, along with codes of conduct and other materials, yet many business schools have only recently formalized their offerings in business ethics. Ethical issues are taught in many areas of the current business-school curriculum, but most explicitly in conjunction with business environment. A lively interplay between these two fields has developed, partially as a result of interpersonal links and a new willingness of scholars in management and in philosophy to communicate at joint professional meetings and to collaborate.

As we approach the 1990s, two kinds of fundamental problems seem to need to be addressed in the context of business environment and business ethics. First, there are the basic economic questions, requiring both economic and normative analysis. These have to do with changes in world trade relationships, with the apparent declining competitiveness of the United States, with the issue of productivity, with questions on what national policies should be developed to cover both manufacturing and high technology. The second set of issues concerns the worker in the workplace—the appropriateness and legality of drug testing, AIDS in the workplace, the availability of flexible work schedules, the position of work organizations in relation to families, the advisability and feasibility of increased benefits to facilitate family responsibilities (such as parental leave), genetic testing, and other issues relating to personal lifestyle and privacy of workers. These questions assume increasing importance as we enter a demographic stage where, again, work organizations will need to develop their strategies to attract qualified employees, since there will be proportionately fewer workers entering the work force in coming years than there have been during the past fifteen years, when the baby-boomers competed for jobs. For managers, understanding and responding effectively to environmental and ethical issues, and anticipating these issues whenever possible, become of greater and greater importance.

THE EVOLUTION OF BUSINESS ENVIRONMENT AS A FIELD

The business-environment field is unusual in the extent to which reflection on its development has occurred on a periodic basis, the most recent being Preston's *Social Issues and Public Policy in Business and Management: Retrospect and Prospect* (1986). Although some classic works date from the 1930s, scholarship in the field began to emerge as a distinct area of theory and empirical research as management itself matured as a discipline during the 1950s. Study of the social, political, legal, and economic environment of business was recognized as essential in the education of future managers by the mid to late 1950s, when the curriculum of the business school was given intense scrutiny in connection with projects undertaken by the American Assembly of Collegiate Schools of Business, the Carnegie Foundation, and the Ford Foundation.

Among business practitioners, opinions were being expressed that a shared commitment to certain basic values and to the integrity of the market economy was vital for a free-enterprise system to function effectively. And yet there was recognition that market failures happen, that certain social needs may go unmet in a market economy, that externalities do occur, and that the legitimacy of business may decline as a result. This recognition, combined with the new social problems that followed the affluence of the 1950s, increased interest in the external environment of the firm. The civil rights movement, the antiwar movement, the environmental movement, the consumer movement, and the women's movement all posed basic questions about the role of business in society. The problems of cities, of universities, of minorities, of youth, of the elderly, and of other demographic and economic subgroups of society commanded a great deal of public and political attention. The organization of public-interest groups, legislative action, and judicial processes all created rapid changes in the environment in which business existed. As a result, management as a discipline had to expand its range of concerns beyond internal processes to the external environment. This new subdiscipline became established in business schools mainly in the 1960s and the 1970s. Scholars in the field were instrumental in forming the Social Issues in Management Division of the Academy of Management when the academy divisionalized in 1971. Early presidents of the division include Sumner Marcus, Lynn Peters, Walter Klein, and William Frederick.

The business-environment field derives from several theoretical traditions. George Steiner (1973) has suggested that several fairly independent, yet sometimes intertwining areas of thought and research came together in response to the new social and managerial problems of the 1960s and 1970s. He presents the metaphor of a multirooted tree with many relatively distinct theoretical lifelines. These lifelines stem largely from the social sciences—which form the intellectual environment within which management developed as a theoretical tradition—from economics, political science, sociology, and also from applied ethics.

Theorists in economics had long discussed the role of business in society, the question of bigness versus smallness in business enterprise, the desirability/necessity of government control, and similar issues. Even when economics as a discipline moved sharply toward the quantitative approach during the 1950s and 1960s, these social issues remained the object of intense public-policy debates and popular interest. Within the university, they tended to migrate to management, to be dealt with in courses such as "Business and Society" at the University of Minnesota, "Competition and Public Policy" at Boston College, "The Philosophy of Enterprise Control" at UCLA, "Industrial Organization and Public Policy" at the University of Illinois, or "The Economics of Poverty" at Stanford.

The discipline of political science was undergoing its own methodological maturation during this same period (roughly 1960–1970). The essay tradition was being supplanted by quantitative analysis of relatively focused questions. Larger scale macro issues, although of great interest among journalists and in the popular imagination of the day, were less amenable to the methodological rigor newly fashionable in the field. Again, a whole set of public-policy issues and options came to be available for academic thought and discussion. And management again provided a hospitable environment within the university through courses such as "Government and Business Enterprise" at the University of Minnesota, "Private Enterprise and Public Policy" at the University of Southern California, and "Business Enterprise and Public Policy" at Cornell University.

Sociology, too, experienced intense internal conflict during the 1960s. Ideological disagreements were becoming increasingly divisive. Schools of business became a place where social issues could be discussed within a less confrontational and more constructive framework than in many departments of sociology. Social problems, customarily covered by sociology, were addressed in courses like "Social Problems of Business" at Carnegie-Mellon University and "Contemporary Issues and Management Responsibility" at Boston College. Special courses dealing with the business community's responsibility in urban problems and the problems of minorities and women were offered in a number of business schools.

The "good government" tradition, going back to the days of anti-trust legislation and the reform of municipal administration in the late 1800s, also became a part of the field. Even today, the spirit of this tradition is often reflected directly or indirectly in values expressed and issues chosen for research. Protection of society from large corporate interests, looking out for the welfare of the common citizen—these are values that continue to appear in the body of knowledge in this field. The tendency of scholars to suggest, sometimes to assume, that proper government policies, programs, or reforms will suffice to solve management problems or social problems derived from business action derives from the "good government" tradition.

After World War II, scholars attempted to understand the role of the corporation in modern society, and their efforts, too, influenced business studies as a whole, this subdiscipline in particular. This type of inquiry was the subject of Drucker's early works, rooted in the actual structure and function of the modern corporation. In *The Future of Industrial Man* (1965), Drucker concluded that the corporation was the main building block of modern industrial society, suggesting that in such a society individual freedom could only be realized through industrial organization: "Power in and over the plant is the basis of social rule and power in an industrial world" (1965: 207). And in *The Concept of the Corporation* (1972), Drucker's classic study of General Motors identified the corporation as a social institution, a line of thought that in some ways anticipated and formed the basis of current delineations of the corporation as both a social system in itself ("corporate culture") and as a building block in organizational society.

The first generation of major textbooks in the field dates from the early to mid-1960s (McGuire 1963; Davis and Blomstrom 1966). For almost a decade, government control over business expanded rapidly. The political demand for public-policy responses to the problems created by business (e.g., externalities or uncompensated social costs), the rising social expectations of many groups (e.g., Blacks, women), and the increasing mobilization of interest groups (e.g., environmentalists, consumers) prompted the establishment of a number of new government agencies. The most important of these were the EEOC (Equal Employment Opportunity Commission), the EPA (Environment Protection Agency), OSHA (Occupational Safety and Health Administration), and the CPSC (Consumer Products Safety Commission), all of which were in place by the early 1970s. Many theorists in the field assumed that the expansion of government control over business would continue indefinitely.

Another tendency of the field became the constant impulse of many of its scholars to take on topical issues and subjects for research. The tragic 1982 cyanide poisonings involving Tylenol, the 1984 Union Carbide disaster at Bhopal, India, and more recently the 1986 mismanagement at NASA that evidently contributed to the Challenger explosion—these and other similar catastrophes are fertile ground in the business-environment/business-ethics field. Whenever a newsworthy event relates to the social, technological, and moral impact of business on the community, the odds are high that one or several business-environment/business-ethics scholars will take it on as a research project. As a result, the work presented at meetings and in published form is sometimes quasi-journalistic, which has advantages and disadvantages. The plus side is that this work can have high social significance—relevance in this field has never been the drawback that it sometimes is when methodological elegance is the dominant criterion by which works are judged. However, some problems have resulted from the topical-issue approach. Cumulative knowledge is hard to define—shifting from topical issue to topical issue provides a fascinating potpourri of riveting incidents to discuss, but hardly adds up to a theoretical framework. The field becomes vulnerable to charges of methodological deficits. But the prevailing philosophy seems to be that definition of a central problem is the primary component of significant work, that methods should help scholars understand research problems rather than constrain them unduly in their choice of topics, and that a certain degree of methodological softness is tolerable. Having said that, it should be mentioned that considerable methodological sophistication is now evident in the field.

THE EVOLUTION OF BUSINESS ETHICS AS A FIELD

The evolution of management as a coherent and intellectually credible field was accompanied by increasing interest in business ethics. Writing in the University of Chicago's *Journal of Business*, Duddy published an article that appears strangely prescient (1945). He pointed out that, for businessmen, the exercise of individual rights brings about corresponding obligations to the society that guarantees these rights. Furthermore, he terms "naive" the belief that the public good will best be served when each individual promotes to the limit his own self-interest (1945: 71). He goes on to suggest such operational features as company codes of ethics and public representation on policymaking boards of corporations—both still topics of discussion in the 1980s.

Donald K. David, Dean of the Graduate School of Business Administration at Harvard University, expressed a similar point of view in speeches delivered at the Economic Club of Detroit, the Harvard Club, the Harvard Business School Club, and Washington and Lee University, later published in the *Harvard Business Review* (1949). Born of the post-World War II competition between democracy and totalitarianism, his philosophy cast business leadership as a bulwark of democratic society and recommended that three qualities be fostered in the business-school curriculum: competent management of business activity; development and application of social skills to make the business enterprise a good society; and willingness to participate constructively in the broader affairs of the community and the nation.

Ethics had been a basic part of those college and university curricula developing in the early decades of the century, when a chief mission of higher education was to imbue graduates with the moral qualities that would enable them to be responsible citizens. But soon, technical skills came to be more emphasized in the business schools, both in scientific management and, perhaps to a somewhat lesser extent, in the developing specialty of human relations. Yet some ethicists maintained a keen interest in business and professional applications. For example, Taeusch's seminal work, *Policy and Ethics in Business* (1931), had provided an ethical underpinning for a searching examination of the role of business in society. And so it was that the concerns of ethicists, philosophers, and theologians were centrally represented in these formative years of the 1940s and 1950s.

An influential set of articles appeared in the *Harvard Business Review* in the 1950s, including works by Boulding (1952), Ohmann (1955; 1957), Demos (1955), Campbell (1957), Johnson (1957), and Broehl (1958). The basic theme of much of this work is the necessity for the individual to integrate personal values and managerial action. On a more general level, the idea was presented that social responsibility should be a guiding principle for corporations. As Demos put it, "Some balance must be struck between profits and social responsibility" (1955: 41). A counterpoint was provided, also in the *Harvard Business Review*, by Levitt in his still-cited "The Dangers of Social Responsibility" (1958), in which he questioned the extent to which business should be encouraged to define public policy questions and answers. The point here is simply that the social responsibility of the corporation was coming to be an important topic in the management literature and a focus of both philosophical and pragmatic argument in the university as well as among the intellectual leaders within the business community.

During this same period the American Assembly of Collegiate Schools of Business (AACSB) sponsored a meeting of business school deans at Arden House, Columbia University's conference center. The resulting report, known informally as Arden House Proceedings and more formally as *Faculty Requirements and Standards in Collegiate Schools of Business*, contained a rough blueprint for the modern business school curriculum. In one section of the report, Nice and Turner recommended that "increasing attention [should be] given to . . . courses in business-government relationships and the social responsibilities of business" (1955: 150). The observation was made that the purpose of an economy is not just to produce material goods but also to attain social beliefs and moral ends, rather a new philosophy to be expressed by business school deans. This viewpoint has been an enduring theme for the past thirty years. During these decades, business education has become both more general and more theoretical and yet, paradoxically, in many respects more technical and more quantitatively focused. Questions relating to business ethics have persisted at a rather subdued level of scholarly concern throughout this period, inspiring intense interest in a particular functional field when some ethical issue arises, subsiding when problems abate, only to resurface in a neighboring functional area when the next scandal occurs.

1959: THE YEAR OF THE REPORTS

The year 1959 was critical for the development of the modern business-school curriculum. The Gordon-Howell report, *Higher Education for Business*, prepared under the sponsorship of the Ford Foundation, made recommendations for the inclusion of more general, integrative, and value-oriented topics to "impress upon the student the multifarious and changing ways in which business interacts with its institutional environment, and, second, to develop in him a sharpened interest in and a sense of responsibility for the kind of society in which he will live and work" (1959: 267). The Pierson report, sponsored by the Carnegie Foundation, presented a similar concept in language that today seems strangely familiar, advocating the need for the manager to "understand, and be sensitive to, the entire economic, political, and social environment in which he will live and in which his business will operate and be judged" (1959: 323). The phrase "economic, political, and social environment" lives on, of course, in the accreditation standards of the American Assembly of Collegiate Schools of Business (AACSB) as its criterion b, in which it mandates inclusion of this area, along with business ethics, in the business school curriculum.

By the beginning of the 1960s the movement to include business and society courses in business curricula was about the magnitude of a noticeable ripple in a sea of traditional functional courses now capped by the more integrative business policy course. Davis posed the question, "Can Business Afford to Ignore Social Responsibilities?" (1960), while Frederick reviewed "The Growing Concern Over Business Responsibility" (1960) and Cheit tackled the question of

"Why Managers Cultivate Social Responsibility" (1964). Texts began to appear for this embryonic field. Eells and Walton's *Conceptual Foundations of Business* (1962) provided a theoretical foundation. McGuire's *Business and Society* (1963) was the first real text widely used for undergraduate courses. Davis and Blomstrom's *Business and Its Environment* (1966) appeared shortly thereafter and continues to be reissued in new editions, now co-authored by Davis and Frederick.

The parameters of the field were defined at this time through several main intellectual sources. At Columbia University some seminal work was being done under the leadership of Clarence Walton and Richard Eells. Their *Conceptual Foundations of Business* (1962) provided a theoretical basis for the field that continues to be relevant today. Their seminars, research, and writing, and the work of their graduate students, provided an enduring theoretical and empirical basis for the newly defined field. The issues and themes addressed in *The Business System* (Walton and Eells: 1967) remain current: the profit motive, entrepreneurship, competition, inflation, government regulation, employment issues, governance, values, ideology, power, pluralism, technology, innovation, and social responsibility.

During this same period, on the West Coast, the business-and-society field was evolving rapidly at the University of California at Berkeley under the leadership of Dow Votaw. A course entitled "Political and Social Environment of Business" was taught for the first time in 1959, with Earl F. Cheit and Dow Votaw sharing teaching and course-development responsibilities. This became a required course for undergraduates, while "Political, Social and Legal Environment" was added to the MBA core curriculum.

Votaw has discussed several dimensions of the development of the field at Berkeley. An eclectic set of perspectives—vaguely philosophical, conceptually historical, frequently hortatory/normative, strongly derivative from business law—gave way to a largely descriptive and case-oriented view in the early 1970s, which in turn evolved into model building and empirical testing around the beginning of the 1980s. Emphasis moved from the macro, or cultural, level to the more micro, or strategic, level, with public policy and political economy gaining importance as integrating concepts. Another change involved academic orientation and faculty background. In the formative years of the Berkeley group—the 1950s and early 1960s—both Cheit and Votaw shared a background of training in law, as does

Edwin Epstein, current chairman of the Program in Business and Social Policy. However, the group became increasingly diverse in the mid-1960s and later, when the faculty came to include members such as Lee Preston, whose background was mainly in economics, S. Prakash Sethi, who brought more of an international business orientation, and, more recently, David Vogel, with his political science background (Votaw 1986).

At UCLA, under the leadership of George Steiner and Neil Jacoby, there has also been considerable interest in this area of study. From 1971 to 1979, faculty development conferences were sponsored by the General Electric Foundation at UCLA and at other locations, including Catholic University, Columbia University, Berkeley, and SUNY-Buffalo. Many of today's instructors came to the discipline from different areas of management, even from the other social sciences, receiving their orientation to the field through these faculty development conferences or through the AACSB summer conferences that came after them, in the years 1979 to 1985. Also on the West Coast, at Stanford University, the field received a good deal of attention, much of it from the graduate-student population, among whom the National Affiliation of Concerned Business Students was established under the leadership of Kirk Hanson.

At Arizona State, Keith Davis was active in developing a way of conceptualizing the field, a model expressed in his 1965 presidential address to the Academy of Management, "The Public Role of Management." Davis was also consulting editor for McGraw-Hill and supported the publication of McGuire's *Business and Society* (1963). Davis and Blomstrom published *Business and Its Environment* (1966), which continues to be reissued in new editions, now co-authored by Davis and Frederick and entitled *Business and Society* (1984).

At the University of Washington in the early 1960s, economics courses and faculty moved out of the business school, leaving behind a nucleus of faculty trained in economics and law that formed the first well-defined graduate program in business and its environment around 1963. Courses in "Business Cycles" (left behind at the business school by economics presumably because of the word "business" in the title), "Business and Society," "The Social Responsibilities of Business," and a number of other business/government/society topics were developed by a faculty that numbered up to fifteen. Joseph McGuire of this department presented a television series on "Business and Society" and, as noted above, published the first textbook by that name in 1963. Sumner Marcus, also of this department, was elected the first president of the Social Issues in Management Division of the Academy of Management when it was formed in 1971.

The climate of the times freed business schools to give social, political, and ethical questions a place in the curriculum. The level of popular discontent with business institutions grew enormously, particularly among those in university settings, students and faculty alike. The obstinacy of business when faced with challenges from the civil rights movement, its seeming complacency with regard to its involvement in the war in Viet Nam, the extent to which business damaged the environment and wasted scarce resources, its obliviousness to the interests of women and of consumers—these perceptions all contributed to widespread demands that business and managers become more socially responsible and subject to more government controls. By the end of the 1960s, Votaw and Sethi were positing "Do We Need a New Corporate Response to a Changing Social Environment?" (1969). Their answer was, of course, in the affirmative. We should note that both McGuire's *Business and Society* (1963) and the Votaw and Sethi two-part article received the McKinsey Award for making an outstanding contribution to the field of management in their respective years. The Academy of Management had also given recognition to works in the field, naming Eells and Walton's *Conceptual Foundations of Business* (1962), McGuire's *Business and Society* (1963), and Davis and Blomstrom's *Business and Its Environment* (1966) as among the best management books published in their respective years. Without question, this area had been acknowledged as a subdiscipline by the end of the 1960s, and, after 1971, the Social Issues in Management Division of the Academy of Management provided an organizational home for scholars in the field.

Reviews of the field began to appear in the early 1970s. A survey sponsored by the National Affiliation of Concerned Business Students indicated that 186 graduate business schools were offering courses in the area (1974). Hanson reviewed the various approaches being used, including course titles and texts (1973). Focusing on practicing managers, Ackerman reviewed "How Companies Respond to Social Responsibility" (1973), while Andrews asked, "Can the Best Corporations be Made Moral?" (1973). Thomas McMahon, C.S.V., an ethicist from Loyola University of Chicago, working at the Center for the Study of Applied Ethics at the Colgate Darden Graduate School of Business Administration at the University of Virginia, did a comprehensive overview of the field. In 1975 his *Report on the Teaching of Socio-Ethical Issues in Collegiate Schools of Business/Public Administration* was issued. Of the 550 colleges and universities responding to McMahon's survey, about 30 percent of the undergraduate and 57 percent of the graduate schools offered a course that included socio-ethical issues. More significantly, for more than 60 percent of the respondents reporting this as either a required or an elective course in the business curriculum, the topic had been introduced within the previous five years. Courses dealing with socio-ethical issues were indeed a new and growing development in the curriculum.

Also around 1975, the Governance Committee of the Social Issues in Management Division of the Academy of Management issued *Business and Society Curriculum: A Position Paper* (1976), suggesting guidelines and resources for course development in the area. During the same period, the AACSB Educational Innovation Committee called attention to the growth of new societal and governmental expectations of corporations and managers. The managerial response to increased public concern and regulatory conditions was seen as an important emerging aspect of business education. At that same time an AACSB task force of scholars in the field of business environment/public policy was formed to study the area and to define the various themes and topics being presented in these courses and felt by the business community to be needed. The AACSB task force and the Curriculum Development Committee of the Social Issues in Management Division of the Academy of Management cooperated in this effort, as the foreword to the summary of the three-part Buchholz report indicates (1979).

Also in 1975, Earl Cheit gave a major address to the annual meeting of the AACSB, "What Is the Field of Business and Society and Where Is It Going?" Operational strategy, rather than the basic legitimacy of the field, was now the focus of attention. Guidance came from the Governance Committee of the Social Issues in Management Division of the Academy of Management and from the AACSB's Standard IV(b). William C. Frederick published a paper entitled "Business and Society Curriculum: Suggested Guidelines for Accreditation" in the *AACSB Bulletin* footnoting, "this paper represents a consensus of the Governance Committee...." (1977:13). He suggested that a threshold course, integrative, broadly conceived, and interdisciplinary in orientation, be offered as part of the required curriculum.

The Buchholz report (1979), a product of the AACSB's interest, did a great deal to provide direction for the field during its next phase of development. This was a period during which most business schools undertook to offer a course in business environment, although the variety of names used for courses and the diversity of topics and teaching approaches remained great.

In 1980, the Committee for Education in Business Ethics of the American Philosophical Association issued a report. Interestingly, this group initially set out to define two sets of curricula, one for philosophy courses and one for business courses. But this initial objective came to be modified, resulting in a single approach being developed. This approach, according to the report, was received rather more favorably by philosophy departments than by business schools. Perhaps this was inevitable, given the origins of the report and the process by which it was evolved. That same year, an influential report appeared under the sponsorship of the Hastings Center, *Ethics in the Education of Business Managers* (Powers and Vogel 1980). Fifth in a series dealing with ethics in various educational and professional programs, it reviewed business-ethics instruction and suggested appropriate approaches, resources, and materials. The overlapping content of business ethics and management practice was a theme, although the tension between the philosophy-oriented and the management-oriented sides of the discipline was acknowledged. In fact, this period saw a growing divergence between these orientations. Now, roughly ten years later, it may be time for a reintegration of these two intellectual traditions.

Beginning in 1986, the Society for Business Ethics began holding its annual meetings just prior to the Academy of Management meetings in order to facilitate cross-attendance. Yet the two approaches to business ethics remain strikingly different in several respects. It is probably fair to say that the philosophers tend to be more rigorous in the theoretical, logical, abstract dimensions of business-ethics problems, while the management-oriented scholars have a greater familiarity with the practical aspects of managerial decisionmaking and the concrete details of the firms and industries being analyzed. Stylistic differences also mark the two disciplines. The philosophers incline to precise definition of terms, elaborate theoretical foundations for problems, and presentations that consist of papers literally being read. Management scholars, on the other hand, are more likely to focus on the pragmatic issues of a particular problem, skimming over fine semantic distinctions, and to present papers in a more discursive format. Given the strong differences in intellectual traditions, analytic modes, and discipline styles and cultures, the extent of *rapprochement* occurring between the two groups in recent years is rather significant.

Yet another development has occurred in business schools and in the business community that merits attention in business environment. Cultural differences in individuals and organizations, the activities of multinational corporations, appropriate technology, and other similar topics have long been a part of the material covered. However, in the 1970s, the AACSB mandated the internationalization of the business-school curriculum. This renewed and expanded interest in international and cross-cultural issues has brought a new set of theoretical and empirical questions to business environment. This part of the curriculum is one of the areas best equipped to handle the complex issues and value-based questions characteristic of international or global business.

THE CHANGING CLIMATE OF BUSINESS ENVIRONMENT

Issues in the field have changed substantially since its beginnings. In the formative years, the 1960s, business was looked upon as a strong institution—so strong that it could be and, more arguably, should be a major instrument for the resolution of various social problems.

The desirability of increased government control over business was also assumed, not so much in the works that form the theoretical base for the field (e.g., Eells and Walton 1962; Walton and Eells 1967), but more so in the first generation of texts appearing in the 1960s and 1970s (e.g., McGuire 1963; Davis and Blomstrom 1966; Steiner 1971). There was fairly widespread consensus in the social sciences at the time that economic development through the industrial and post-industrial stages would necessarily lead to increasing institutionalization of a variety of social needs in the public sector. It was well into the beginning of the 1970s before serious questions were posed about the appropriateness of the Scandinavian-type model as a prototype for modern Western democracies. The recent trends toward deregulation and privatization were then hardly discernible in academic circles, although their philosophical and economic bases had been formulated. The intellectual vigor of the neoconservative movement, widespread dissatisfaction with the implementation of some of the more ambitious domestic plans hatched by the federal government in the 1960s, and the impossibility of expanding government commitments and responsibilities during the recessionary times that followed the oil crisis of the early 1970s—all these factors combined to bring about a new questioning of the inclination to rely on the federal government for solutions to society's problems. The past ten years have brought about deregulation in many key areas of the economy. We now have a celebration of the potential of private enterprise, acting unfettered by excessive federal regulation, to produce the economic resources that permit increased opportunities for personal achievement and economic growth.

In the field of business environment, the mood has also shifted, looking with more sympathy at the problems of the private sector in the past decade. During the earlier years, there was an inclination to assume the economic viability of business, and the central issues of the field tended to revolve around questions of legitimacy and justice. Now more emphasis is placed on the performance of business in an increasingly competitive world economy. The capacity of the business community to respond effectively to social issues is no longer the single central focus. New concerns are the ability of American business to innovate, to implement new technologies, to manage work-force costs and to improve productivity. From the public-policy viewpoint, important topics are the management of fiscal and monetary policy to create conditions favorable for economic growth, the modification of antitrust policy to allow domestic industry to compete with the cooperative industrial groupings of other nations, and the encouragement of innovation in the U.S. economy. Still remaining as real human problems are issues such as retirement policies, job training for the disadvantaged, the disinvestment of American business in many American communities, and the problems of women and minorities, as well as personnel issues such as privacy—particularly genetic, AIDS, and drug testing in the workplace—employment at will, and executive liability.

During the early 1970s, abundance and just distribution were seen as critical issues in the study of the U.S. economic system and the social responsibility of business. Just distribution remains a concern, now on a global scale, but the assumption of continued abundance has been shattered by a decade of economic uncertainty. New ideas from the neoconservative philosophers have strongly challenged the liberal tradition that has dominated in academe, even in business schools, for the past five decades. The appeal of the quasi-socialist systems of the Scandinavian nations has been replaced by the allure of the successful Japanese system (perhaps also a variant type of quasi-socialism), with the "free-enterprise" pockets such as Singapore and South Korea looming on the intellectual horizon.

CHAPTER 2

The Business/Government/Society Relationship in Management Thought

Rogene A. Buchholz

This chapter describes the major conceptual developments that have attempted to link business, government, and society, with a primary, but not exclusive, focus on the social and political (noneconomic) aspects of the business environment. The concepts of social responsibility, social responsiveness, public policy, and business ethics have been the major paradigms by which business/government/ society linkages have been studied, and they continue to provide a focus and framework for the field. Newer developments relate to strategic planning and environmental analysis of threats and opportunities, and these approaches will also be considered.

The field of business environment developed as a response to the major noneconomic issues that became important in the 1960s as society turned its attention to social questions such as equal opportunity, pollution control, consumer protection, and so forth. Existing courses in business schools were based primarily on an economic paradigm. Social issues did not fit into the economic framework based on free-market principles and so could not be addressed in these courses. Thus, new courses needed to be developed and incorporated into the curriculum to deal with these issues. Basic economic analyses were refined as the assumptions of free-market economics were examined critically from a societal viewpoint. The social costs and collectively shared benefits of business, along with cost/benefit analysis of governmental actions such as regulation, also came to be treated in this area of the curriculum. These courses, which initially were taught by faculty from the existing fields of management, eventually developed into a separate field with a fairly specific body of knowledge and a core of scholars and faculty expressly trained in business environment.

SOCIAL RESPONSIBILITY

The field went by various names: "Business and Society," "The Changing Environment of Business," "Business and Public Policy," "The Social, Political, and Legal Environment of Business," and other titles suggesting the integrative and interactive dimensions of the subject. The concept of social responsibility was the initial paradigm to provide some degree of integration and a foundation for the field. While this concept had many definitions, some common elements provided a core of meaning. First, there was the idea that a private corporation has responsibilities that go beyond the production of goods and services at a profit—specifically, a responsibility to help society solve some of its most pressing social problems. Another observation was that a corporation must serve a broader constituency than stockholders alone—there are various groups of stakeholders, including employees, customers, and stockholders, to which the corporation must respond. Third was the notion that corporations relate to society in ways that are external to marketplace transactions and so must take these nonmarket impacts into account. Finally, there was the position that corporations serve a wider range of human values than the traditional economic values that are exclusively dominant when the corporation is viewed solely as an economic institution.

The debate about social responsibility was extensive. The supporters of social responsibility as an extraeconomic goal of business maintained that business must accommodate itself to social change if it expects to survive, that it must take a long-run or enlightened view of self-interest and help solve social problems to create a better environment for itself, that it can gain a better public image by being socially responsible, that government regulation can be avoided if business can meet changing social expectations before issues become politicized, that business has enormous resources that would be useful in solving social problems, that social problems can be turned into profitable business opportunities, and that business has a moral obligation to help solve social problems that it has created or perpetuated rather than dumping these problems on society.

But there were counterarguments stressing that business in a market system must fulfill its primary economic objectives. From this perspective, economic performance *is* social responsibility. The extra-economic definition of social responsibility, it was said, provided no mechanism for accountability of the use of corporate resources, even though managers were legally and ethically bound to earn the highest possible rate of return on stockholder's equity (Friedman 1970). It was also argued that social responsibility, if defined by large corporations, could pose a threat to the pluralistic nature of our society (Levitt 1958). Another assertion in this vein was that business executives have little experience or incentive to solve social problems (Keim and Meiners 1978). The inference was that government officials are charged with this responsibility, should exercise their authority in these directions, and can be held accountable. Finally, social responsibility was represented as a fundamentally subversive doctrine, that, if taken seriously, would undermine the foundations of a free-enterprise system (Friedman 1962).

After the smoke began to clear from this debate, it was clear to both proponents and opponents of corporate social responsibility (as defined by the first, more "liberal" tradition) that there were certain key issues that had not, and perhaps could not, be settled. One concerned the operational definition of social responsibility. How should a corporation's resources be allocated to help solve social problems? With what specific problems should a given corporation concern itself? What priorities should be established? Does social responsibility refer to company actions taken to comply with the law or only to those voluntary actions that go beyond legal requirements? What goals or standards of performance would be adequate? What measures should be used to determine if a corporation is socially responsible or socially irresponsible?

The traditional marketplace provided little or no information to the manager that would be useful in making decisions about solving social problems. But the concept of social responsibility was no more helpful. Given this lack of precision, corporate executives who wanted to be socially responsible were left to follow their own values and interests or some rather vague generalizations about changing social values and new expectations.

Another key problem was that the concept of social responsibility did not take into account the competitive environment in which corporations function. Many advocates of social responsibility treated the corporation as an isolated entity with an unlimited ability to engage in unilateral social action. But it came to be increasingly recognized that corporations are severely limited in their ability to respond to social problems. If a firm unilaterally engages in social action that increases its costs and prices, it will place itself at a competitive disadvantage relative to other firms in the industry that may not share its commitment. Action to solve social problems is not feasible in a competitive system unless all competitors pursue roughly the same policy on the same problems. Since collusion among competitors is illegal, the only way such concerted action can occur is when some other institution, such as government, makes all competitors engage in the same activity and follow the same policy. Chamberlain makes this argument as follows:

> Every business . . . is, in effect, "trapped" in the business system that it has helped to create. It is incapable, as an individual unit, of transcending that system. . . . The dream of the socially responsible corporation that replicated over and over again can transform our society is illusory. . . . Because their aggregate power is not unified, not truly collective, not organized, they [corporations] have no way, even if they wished, of redirecting that power to meet the most pressing needs of society. . . . Such redirection could only occur through the intermediate agency of government rewriting the rules under which all corporations operate. (Chamberlain 1973: 4, 6)

The debate about social responsibility never took this institutional context of corporations seriously. Yet all the while the debate about social responsibility was continuing and corporate executives were asking for a definition of their social responsibilities, government was in fact rewriting the rules under which all corporations operate in a vast amount of legislation and regulation pertaining especially to the physical environment, occupational safety and health, equal opportunity, and consumer concerns.

The last unresolved issue concerns the moral underpinnings of the notion. "Responsibility" is a moral term that implies an obligation to someone or something. It is clear that business has an economic responsibility to produce goods and services and perform other economic functions for society. But why does business have social responsibilities as well? The debate produced no generally accepted moral principle that would impose upon business an obligation to work for social betterment (Frederick 1978). Various moral structures were proposed to establish this obligation, such as business survival, enlightened self-interest, responsible use of power, corporate citizenship, and similar generalizations. The opponents of social responsibility such as Levitt and Friedman fared little better in this regard, although they raised the arguments of preserving free enterprise, enhancing productivity, resisting government interference in private decisions, and all the rest. Such moralistic debate generates a good deal of heat but little light. The absence of a clear moral principle supporting the notion of corporate social responsibility is perhaps the most fundamental problem with the concept.

CORPORATE SOCIAL RESPONSIVENESS

The intractability of these issues, according to one author, "posed the dreadful possibilities that the debate over corporate social responsibility would continue indefinitely with little prospect of final resolution or that it would simply exhaust itself and collapse as a viable legitimate question" (Frederick 1978: 5). But beginning in the 1970s, a theoretical and conceptual reorientation began to take place regarding the corporation's response to the social environment. This new approach was labelled "corporate social responsiveness." Initially, it appeared that only semantics were involved, but it gradually became apparent that the shift from responsibility to responsiveness was much more substantive, representing an attempt to escape the unresolved dilemmas that had emerged from the social-responsibility debate. The concept of corporate social responsiveness was defined by one author as follows:

> Corporate social responsiveness refers to the capacity of a corporation to respond to social pressures. The literal act of responding, or of achieving a generally responsive posture, to society is the focus of corporate social responsiveness. . . . One searches the organization for mechanisms, procedures, arrangements, and behavioral patterns that, taken collectively, would mark the organization as more or less capable of responding to social pressures. It then becomes evident that organizational design and managerial competence play important roles in how extensively and how well a company responds to social demands and needs. (Frederick 1978: 6)

The focus of the field was thus redirected to the external environment as the boundary for the field and to a managerial orientation that placed the subject matter squarely in the business-school curriculum. Social issues were discussed in the context of management policy. A body of knowledge began to emerge that could be taught and extended by research into issues and concerns related to corporate policy and structure.

Research focused on internal corporate responsiveness to social problems. For example, Ackerman and Bauer (1976) developed a conceptual model that outlined three stages of the internal response process: awareness, commitment, and implementation. In the first stage, the chief executive officer recognizes the importance of a social problem. This awareness is marked by several activities, including speeches, special projects, and an overall company policy. Stage two entails the appointment of a staff specialist to coordinate the company's responses to the problem. In the third phase, the whole organization becomes involved. A particular social-policy objective is made a goal for all managers in the organization, reinforced by reward systems, performance measurement, and other institutional processes.

This initial research by Ackerman and Bauer triggered other models of the corporate response process. For example, Sethi (1975) also developed a three-stage model, which defined corporate behavior as social obligation, social responsibility, and social responsiveness. In the first stage, social obligation, the corporation seeks legitimacy by meeting legal and economic criteria only. The corporation believes it is accountable only to its stockholders and strongly resists any regulation of its activities. In the second stage, social responsibility, the corporation recognizes the limited relevance of meeting only legal and economic requirements and adopts a broader set of criteria, including a social dimension, for measuring its performance. Management considers groups other than stockholders that might be affected by its actions and is willing to work with these outside groups for good environmental legislation. In the third stage, social responsiveness, the corporation accepts its role as defined by the social system and understands that this role is subject to change over time. Furthermore, it is willing to account for its actions to other groups, even those not directly affected, and assists legislative bodies in developing better legislation. Thus, business becomes an active promoter as well as supporter of environmental and social concerns.

From these examples, it can be seen that the generally accepted notion of corporate social responsiveness relates to how corporations actually respond to social problems. The important questions have become less moral, less concerned with a corporation's responsibility to address social problems, and more pragmatic and action-oriented, dealing with the ability of a corporation to respond and what changes are necessary to enable it to do so more effectively.

An advantage of the social-responsiveness philosophy is its managerial orientation. The concept goes beyond the philosophical debate about responsibility and obligation, focusing on the problems and prospects of making corporations more socially responsive. One of the reasons for research into corporate response patterns is to discover which have proven most effective.

The corporate social-responsiveness approach also lends itself to more rigorous analytical research to discover patterns of response and specific techniques, such as environmental scanning or the social audit, which can improve the response process. Such research can also determine how management can best institutionalize social policy throughout the organization, investigating what organizational structures are most appropriate, whether top-management commitment is crucial, what changes in the reward structure improve the corporation's response to social problems, what role the public-affairs department should play in the response process, and how social policy can be formulated effectively for the organization as a whole (Frederick 1978).

Given these advantages, however, the concept of corporate social responsiveness is still faced with the same key problems that plagued the social-responsibility concept. It does not clarify how corporate resources should be allocated for the solution of social problems. Companies respond to different problems in different ways and to varying degrees, but debates continue over which pattern of responsiveness will produce the greatest amount of social betterment. The philosophy of responsiveness does not help the company decide what problems to get involved in and what priorities to establish. Thus it provides only limited guidance to management, as does social responsibility, on the best strategies or policies to be adopted to produce social betterment. The concept seems to suggest that management itself, by determining the degrees of social responsiveness and the problems it will respond to, decides the meaning of social responsiveness and what social goods and services shall be produced (Frederick 1978).

Social responsiveness does not deal with the institutional context of business much more adequately than did social responsibility. Research has not studied very thoroughly the impact government regulation has made on the corporation and how the corporation has responded to changes in the political environment. Individual institutions have been treated as rather isolated phenomena that could choose a response pattern irrespective of the institutional context in which they operate.

Finally, the question of an underlying moral principle continues to be put aside. Social pressures are assumed to exist, and it is believed that business must respond to them, which places business in a passive role of simply reacting to social change. The concept of social responsiveness provides no compelling moral reason for business to get involved in social problems. An explicit value theory, along with a specific set of values for business to uphold in making social responses, is yet to be developed (Frederick 1978).

THE REALITY OF PUBLIC POLICY

In the mid-seventies, academics and businessmen began to realize that a fundamental change was taking place in the political environment of business—government was engaged in shaping business behavior and making business respond to a wide array of social problems by passing an unprecedented amount of legislation and writing new regulations pertaining to these problems. The political system responded to the social revolution of the 1960s by enacting over 100 new laws regulating business activity during that decade. New regulatory agencies were created or new responsibilities were assigned to old agencies, and these issued thousands of rules and procedural requirements during the 1960s and 1970s. The number of pages in the Federal Register grew from 20,036 in 1970 to 42,422 in 1974. In March 1979, the Office of the Federal Register reported that 61,000 pages of government regulations had been issued for the previous year, a 305 percent increase in eight years.

The new type of social regulation, as it came to be called, affected virtually every department or functional area and every level of management within the corporation. This growth of regulation was referred to as a second managerial revolution, involving a shift of decisionmaking power and control over the corporation from the managers to a vast cadre of government regulators who were influencing, and in many cases controlling, managerial decisions in the typical business corporation. In 1976, for example, a total of eighty-three federal agencies were regulating business in one or another aspect. The types of decisions that were becoming increasingly subject to government intervention are basic to the operation of a business organization (Weidenbaum 1979, 1981).

During the late seventies, more and more attention was paid to this changing political environment. Books were written that provided a comprehensive overview of the effects of government regulation on business (Weidenbaum 1979). Studies were completed that attempted to measure the costs of social regulation to the private sector (Weidenbaum and DeFina, 1978; Arthur Andersen, 1979). The results of this activity indicated that this environment was largely hostile to business, giving rise to legislation and regulation that interfered with the ability of business to perform its basic economic mission. Social regulation was costly, it had negative impacts on productivity, it contributed to inflation, and it diverted management attention from the basic task of running the business.

Management educators began to take public policy seriously during the same period. The regulatory role of government continued to expand until about 1977–78, when the Carter administration moved to streamline regulatory processes in several areas, particularly OSHA. The Reagan campaign of 1979 promised widespread cutbacks in the size and function of many regulatory agencies, a promise kept upon election. Two conferences of business school deans were held, one in 1976 and the other in 1977, which dealt with regulatory reform and public policy respectively. At both meetings many deans expressed the conviction that something new was happening to the role of business in society, and that this deserved attention in course offerings of schools of business and management. Out of these meetings came the idea for a comprehensive study of the area called "Business Environment/Public Policy" that was cosponsored by the American Assembly of Collegiate Schools of Business and the Center for the Study of American Business at Washington University in St. Louis, Missouri (Buchholz 1979). Its purpose was to assess the state of the art in the field and to make recommendations for improvement of teaching and research. Many management educators stated their belief that an improved curriculum in this area was essential if schools were to prepare future managers adequately for the world in which they would be working. While social responsibility and corporate social responsiveness continue to be used as integrating concepts, public policy has provided much of the focus for the field in recent years.

BUSINESS ETHICS

Ethics has to do with a definition of the good life, the broad sense of human welfare, the meaning and purpose of life, the nature of a human community, and similar questions that are basic to human existence. These questions cannot be answered by appeal to an economic calculus such as profit-and-loss or cost-benefit analysis, and yet they are fundamental to any discussion of business's role in society, whether looked at from the standpoint of social responsibility, social responsiveness, or public policy. Society builds and operates institutions, including business, based on its conceptions of the things that make a life worth living. These institutions must necessarily change as society's notions of a good life change. For business to be effective in its response to the social and political environment, it must be motivated to look beyond its own immediate economic self-interest and to recognize the ethical and moral dimensions of the issues being raised.

In the early 1980s, the subject of business ethics received a great deal of increased attention in schools of business and management around the country as well as in corporations themselves. This interest was heralded by the appearance of comprehensive studies in business ethics, most notably Powers and Vogel (1980), the publication of a few initial textbooks on the subject (Beauchamp and Bowie 1979; Donaldson and Werhane 1979; Barry 1979), the establishment of centers and chairs in business ethics, and the development of courses in business ethics at some leading schools of business and management. Since that time, the number of textbooks in business ethics has grown, and more such courses have been established. A survey conducted by the Center for Business Ethics at Bentley College in 1980 found that almost half of the 655 schools of business and management responding to their survey offered a course in business ethics. Of the 338 schools that did not offer a course, 48 planned to do so, and another 144 indicated that they would like to at some time in the future (Hoffman and Moore 1982).

Thus began an explicit focus on the subject of business ethics, not as an add-on or subset of the business-environment and public-policy courses, but as a legitimate subject for business schools in its own right. Several reasons lie behind this development, but in general it indicates some fundamental changes in society regarding a consensus on ethical standards and the conduct of institutions including business organizations. The debate about business ethics reflects the confusion following the upset of previously held notions about how a business ought to act in a market-oriented society. This broader view of the problem is held by Powers and Vogel:

> In our view, the new concern for corporate ethics and managerial ethics is the logical culmination of a series of social transformations through which the connecting tissues that make up the "organic" connection between management, institution, and society have eroded. What constitutes "ethical custom" is evaporating. The ability of the market mechanism to carry the normative freight between corporations and society increasingly turns to other ways to try to connect its changing values to corporate practice (Powers and Vogel 1980: 7).

The authors go on to list four factors they believe have contributed to this erosion of the consensus about appropriate corporate and managerial practice. First, the increased size of corporate institutions has meant that the market does not govern many current corporate activities and decisions—in a sense, corporations have outgrown the market mechanism. Second, there has been a growth in the scope of legal requirements and constraints on business and of governmental involvement in corporate activities. Third, public awareness and concern have developed about the externalities (such as pollution) that are not amenable to direct market control. Last, human dignity and the value of human life are new priorities in the agenda of social values.

Other reasons for the current level of interest in business ethics include the widespread decline of confidence in business leadership as shown by polls of public attitudes. Insider trading, illegal campaign contributions in this country, foreign payments abroad, and other such scandals contribute to this decline and raise questions in the public mind about the degree to which corporate leaders themselves believe in and abide by the rules of the market mechanism. The growth of management as a profession may also contribute to the interest in developing general ethical standards for management. Finally, questions about the legitimacy of the management role, as raised in the ongoing debate about corporate governance, may motivate business managers to find a new ethical justification for their role in society.

According to Powers and Vogel, ethics is concerned with actions that are directed to improving the welfare of people, while ethicists explore the concepts and language that express these actions:

> Some are primarily concerned with the justification of this concern itself, others with the delineation or justification of principles that specify appropriate welfare-meeting conduct, and others with the relationship between these principles and the rules of character traits that guide people toward specific behavior to achieve human welfare. In essence ethics is concerned with clarifying what constitutes human welfare and the kind of conduct necessary to promote it (Powers and Vogel 1980: 1).

Ethical issues in corporate performance can be discussed on at least three levels. At the first level, there is a concern about personal and professional behavior in the context of the market system, focusing on standards of managerial conduct (honesty, trust) that are necessary for the market to function effectively. The second level relates to corporate policy decisions involving questions of social justice, such as equal opportunity, plant closings, pollution control, and workplace safety and health. The third level deals with the moral dimensions of the overall system in which corporations function. Ethical questions at this level include corporate governance, the role of profits, the nature of competition, the role of private property, and similar issues.

The focus on business ethics keeps alive the moral dimension that had been an integral part of the social-responsibility debate, but which had begun to fade with the emphasis on social responsiveness and public policy. With their managerial and policy slants, these latter paradigms made it difficult to deal explicitly with ethical considerations. And yet, there are both dangers and opportunities with this ethical focus. The ethics approach could be used to harass business; business ethicists might take the moral highground and simply criticize business values, actions, and organizations. While business is certainly not above criticism, mere preaching does not add much to our knowledge and understanding of business behavior.

However, business ethics presents an opportunity finally to confront certain key ethical and value questions that have been largely ignored or circumvented up to this point. Ethical considerations are fundamental to define terms like social betterment and the public interest, as well as the missions and purposes of business organizations. The ethical paradigm offers the chance to deal with these questions in an explicit fashion while drawing on a rich body of knowledge and tradition.

STRATEGIC MANAGEMENT

A recent development in the field is the concept of strategic management. Through the use of this framework, environmental analysis can be linked to strategy development. Most textbooks on strategy consider the external environment (economic, technological, social, and political influences) and deal with the threats and opportunities in that environment to which management must respond. Thus the concept integrates environmental concerns into the formulation of strategy for the corporation.

Prior to the development of strategic management, the business-policy course was viewed as the capstone in the typical core curriculum of business schools. With no responsibility to transmit a specific body of knowledge, the business-policy course could concentrate on integrating knowledge that had already been acquired in the functional areas and on developing further the student's skill in using that knowledge (Gordon and Howell 1959). It was believed that this integration would take place by exposing the student to the problems of several functions at one time, typically through the medium of a complex case. No further substance was felt to be necessary to understand the role of the top manager in a business enterprise, the assumption being that all there was to managing was the coordination of the various functional fields, which would somehow lead to appropriate choices about the future of the business organization. The theory was that a firm could be managed through the collected wisdom of the various functional areas and that all top management had to do was pick and choose from among available options.

Two trends in particular have elevated this integration problem to a position of much greater significance than previously. The first is the rapid technological, economic, social, and political change that has affected business organizations. The business environment is much more unstable and complex than it used to be—managing the enterprise is more complicated than in simpler days. The second trend is the variety of changes that have occurred in the organization and structure of business. There has been tremendous growth as firms have expanded into multiple product lines and into multinational and multicultural markets. These increases in size and complexity have been accompanied by changes in the administrative structure and processes by which firms are managed (Schendel and Hofer 1979).

The focus on policy as a means of integrating functional areas thus became somewhat outdated. Questions were raised as to whether integration could really be accomplished without some substantive paradigm for doing it and without going beyond the content of the various functional fields. Thus the concept of strategy was developed to integrate not only functional areas, but also the firm and its environment across several organizational levels. The concept of strategy has proven useful in handling greater organizational complexity amid greater environmental turbulence (Schendel and Hofer 1979).

Strategy refers to the formulation of basic organizational missions, purposes, and objectives, and the policies and programs to achieve them (Wheelen and Hunger 1984). Strategic management has been defined as those managerial decisions and actions that determine the long-run performance of a corporation. The concept encompasses strategy formulation, strategy implementation, and evaluation and control. It therefore emphasizes the monitoring and evaluating of environmental opportunities and constraints with respect to a corporation's strengths and weaknesses.

Strategic management is concerned primarily with relating the organization to its environment, devising strategies to adapt to that environment, and assuring that the implementation of strategies takes place. This involves: (1) surveillance of the changing environment; (2) identification in that environment of opportunities to exploit and dangers to avoid; (3) evaluation of company strengths and weaknesses important in formulating and evaluating strategies; (4) formulating missions and objectives; (5) identifying strategies to achieve company aims; (6) evaluating the strategies and choosing those that will be implemented; and (7) establishing and monitoring processes to make sure that strategies are properly implemented (Steiner and Miner 1982).

The concept of strategic management enables a firm both to anticipate and create the future and to prepare suitable guidelines for making better current decisions. To a large extent, the success of a company will depend on how well it formulates its strategy in light of its evolving environment, how well it defines and articulates its strategy, and how well it assures its implementation. Without this long-run perspective, a company is forced to live from day to day. The elements of the strategic planning process include understanding the changing environment in which a company finds itself, the basic company purposes, long-range planning objectives, and program policies and strategies:

1. The strategic planning process focuses attention on opportunities and threats, but it also asks fundamental questions about the nature and purpose of the organization.

2. The strategic planning process addresses itself to defining the mission of the company. This includes the basic products and/or businesses of the company and the markets in which they are distributed. The basic purposes refer to fundamental aims the company seeks for such factors as product quality, customer service, response to community interests, and ethical conduct.

3. The strategic planning process provides a unified framework within which managers can deal with the major issues managers should face, for dealing with major opportunities, and for assessing strengths that can be capitalized upon and weaknesses that must be addressed. It forces thought processes that are essential to better management. (Steiner and Miner 1982: 29–30).

Thompson and Strickland (1983) identify five phases involved in the job of managing the total enterprise: (1) defining organization purpose and mission; (2) establishing objectives; (3) formulating a strategy; (4) implementing and executing the chosen strategic plan; and (5) evaluating and reformulating the strategic plan according to actual experience, changing conditions, and new priorities. The first three phases constitute the direction-setting function of management and are entrepreneurial in character. The fourth phase embraces all of the managerial tasks and responsibilities associated with putting the plan into place and generating the desired results. The fifth is necessary because changing external conditions, emerging market and competitive developments, and new internal priorities and circumstances combine to make reappraisal of strategy a regular occurrence.

As the strategy concept makes clear, the business organization must take the external environment into account in formulating strategy. According to Wheelen and Hunger (1984), the external environment consists of variables outside the organization that are not typically within the short-run control of top management. These variables form the context within which the corporation exists and must function. There are two categories into which these variables can be classified.

1. Task environment: Those elements or groups that directly affect and are affected by an organization's major operations. Some of these groups are stockholders, governments, suppliers, local communities, competitors, customers, creditors, labor unions, and trade associations. These stakeholders have different interests, some of which may be noneconomic in nature.

2. Societal environment: More general social, political, economic, and technological forces that do not necessarily directly touch upon the activities of the organization, but can, and often do, influence its decisions (Wheelen and Hunger 1984: 7).

The strategy paradigm assumes that the organization takes a proactive stance towards the environment, which recognizes that interactions with the environment will be a two-way street. The paradigm encourages management to initiate interactions with the environment wherever this is possible. But, since the focus remains on the internal actions of the business, the external society remains secondary in importance.

The strategy paradigm places the concerns of the business environment and the public-policy area squarely in the business-school curriculum, eliminating any doubts about the importance to management of considering the impact of environmental factors on the business organization. Strategy carries the managerial orientation a step further than the previous paradigms and provides an explicit framework to use in integrating social and political concerns into the planning process of corporations. The strategy framework also provides a means to analyze the effects of social and political factors on business and to develop appropriate management responses to the threats and opportunities of these factors. And yet, use of the strategy paradigm means that ethical and value issues are largely ignored or at best become peripheral considerations in the development of management strategy, which still is based primarily on technical or economic considerations. Too, cultural, societal, and political processes are examined less fully than they would be in a specific business-environment course.

THE FUTURE

The social and political environments of the corporation have undoubtedly gained importance over the last several years. While the corporation is primarily an economic institution and is likely to remain so for the foreseeable future, its economic functions are no longer as dominant as they traditionally have been and must be studied in relation to the social and political roles that business is assuming. The business institution is being reshaped and is reshaping itself to meet these new responsibilities. These changes call for new theories and models to describe and analyze business/government/society relationships.

> The traditional economic model of business operations has served business well. Business needs to make no apology for its profound role in bringing economic plenty to many parts of the world. The job that business has done ranks high among civilization's all-time achievements. If conditions have changed, however, then the old model may not apply precisely the way it applied in the past. In a dynamic world businessmen are not going to solve tomorrow's problems with yesterday's theories. (Davis and Blomstrom 1976: 14–15)

Business environment is the one area in the business-school curriculum where the relationships of business, government, and society and social and political issues of importance to corporations can be explicitly studied and researched. It has stood alone in most business schools as the area that calls attention to normative issues and that encourages nonquantitative questions and analysis. Thus, its importance in schools of business and management should not be diminished in the future. At present, the existence of many conceptual approaches is more of a strength than a weakness. The social and political phenomena covered by the subject are complex, and multiple approaches are more likely to do this complexity justice.

After some years of growing government regulation, it is clear that a sense of social responsibility is as important as ever. Regulations can be resisted or ignored, they are subject to varying interpretations, they cannot be enforced uniformly without thousands of regulators checking on business, and the emphasis placed on regulation changes with each political administration. Efforts at self-regulation require even more of a sense of social responsibility when business voluntarily assumes social obligations that go beyond its economic mission.

For business to be responsive to social and political concerns requires organizational restructuring. Government regulations, for example, have entailed changes in organizations, where counterparts of regulatory agencies have been created to assure compliance with regulations (Weidenbaum 1981). Changes have also taken place at the board level to incorporate social and political concerns into corporate policy (Sethi, Cunningham, and Miller 1979). Continuing research into organizational variables is vital to determine which will most enable a corporation to be more responsive to the social and political environments.

Despite the recent backlash regarding regulation, government will always have part in determining the rules by which all corporations are expected to operate—it is the appropriate body to formulate public policy for the business system as a whole. Thus, government will most likely continue to set standards where necessary, provide incentives to ensure business compliance, act as an enforcer of last resort, and identify new safety and health hazards. These are just a few of the regulatory roles that government will continue to play in society. Given the centrality of government, it will always be important for business to keep aware of public-policy developments and to look for appropriate ways to influence public-policy outcomes.

For business to be effective in responding to its social and political environments, it must be motivated to look beyond its own immediate economic self-interest and recognize the ethical and value dimensions of the issues being raised. Thus far, business has gotten by on largely economic grounds—raising questions about the cost of regulations, the impact of regulation on economic growth, and the economic constraints of being socially responsible and responsive. It is unlikely that this defensive strategy will continue to work in the future. Social issues involve questions of justice, rights, fairness, equity—all of which are ethical concepts. For business to participate meaningfully in the resolution of these issues, it must learn ethical language and concepts and consider the ethical and moral dimensions of the questions. For business to develop effective strategy, it must weigh ethical and moral factors when defining its mission and purpose.

Corporate strategy allows for the integration of social and political concerns into the planning and policy-making processes of corporate organizations, a problem that has plagued the business-environment and public-policy field since its inception. There will be a continual need to develop better ways of assessing environmental factors and devising effective and appropriate means for coping with the threats and opportunities these factors present. They need to be incorporated into the heart of business policy and planning, in order to have a real impact on organizational and managerial behavior. More research is needed into better and more effective ways to achieve this integration.

The field of business environment defines the changing role of business in society and keeps managers aware of changes in their responsibilities and in the expectations of their various constituencies. As increasing attention is paid to nonmarket aspects of business behavior, research and teaching in business environment make a vital contribution to the development of solutions to emerging problems in the social and political environments of the corporation. New conceptual developments in relating business, government, and society can help prescribe a realistic role for business to play in contributing to the public interest as a socially responsible steward of wealth and creator of social utilities.

Three Current Approaches and Applications in Business Environment

PUBLIC POLICY AS AN INTEGRATING CONCEPT

Rogene A. Buchholz

For business faculty, the political environment initially came into focus through the growth of government regulation in the 1960s and 1970s. Increasingly public policy was used as a paradigm for the field. Unlike its earlier application in traditional business/government courses, the new use of public policy considered values and ethics central to public-policy formulation and concentrated largely on non-economic concerns. Through this concept, social issues became public issues, and social responsibility changed to public responsibility. The public-policy concept brought government directly into the realm of business concerns. Rather than fighting change, which had proved to be a losing battle in many instances, or simply accommodating itself to change, business has now, by and large, adopted a more sophisticated approach. This has been called the proactive stance, since business now attempts to influence change by becoming involved in the public-policy process. Thus business seeks to sway public opinion regarding specific social issues or the free-enterprise system in general and to affect the legislative and regulatory process as to specific laws and regulations.

To coordinate and direct these efforts, a new function has emerged within corporations. Called public-issues management, it involves anticipating issues that may affect the corporation, researching those issues to arrive at a position, and developing strategies to assure that the corporation will have maximum influence on the outcome of the public-policy process.

Academia has responded by putting more public-policy content into its existing business and society or business and government courses. New courses have been instituted that focus explicitly on the public-policy process, government regulation of business, or public-issues management. Research has concentrated on regulatory reform, political-action committees, advocacy advertising, executive liability, lobbying activities, environmental forecasting, and strategic planning.

Public policy has some distinct advantages over the corporate social-responsibility and corporate social-responsiveness concepts that dominated the field earlier. Within its context, few questions are raised about the nature and extent of management's social responsibilities. Once regulations are approved, these responsibilities are spelled out in excruciating detail. The government gets involved in specifying technology, labelling requirements, safety equipment, and the like. Where questions arise about the legality or feasibility of regulations, the court system is available to resolve the issue. Particular health and safety standards, for example, are either struck down or upheld by the courts. Affirmative-action programs are supported or overturned according the court's interpretation of civil rights legislation.

The public-policy focus treats business in its institutional context, advocating that managers learn more about government and the public-policy process so that they can influence it appropriately. Government is recognized as the proper body to formulate and formalize public policy for the society as a whole. Some form of government response to most social issues is believed to be inevitable, and even substantial corporate reform along the lines of corporate social responsibility or corporate social responsiveness may fail to eliminate government involvement in various aspects of business. Government has a legitimate right to determine public policy for corporations in response to changing public expectations.

There is also, at least on the surface, little need for a moral underpinning for a business obligation to produce social betterment. Society makes decisions about the allocation of resources through the public-policy process, which is based on collective notions about social betterment. The result is legislation, with regulations that directly affect business behavior. Business, then, has a moral obligation as a good citizen to obey the law. Failure to do so subjects business and its executives to all sorts of penalties, monetary and otherwise. The social responsibility of business is thus to follow the directives of society at large as expressed in and through the public-policy process.

However, the concept of public policy, which at first glance seemed to eliminate many of the dilemmas associated with social responsibility and social responsiveness, actually may fare no better on closer examination. As business becomes more politically involved in writing the rules of the game or preventing new ones from being written, the question of principles for managerial behavior again becomes relevant. What criteria, other than pure self-interest, should guide the corporation's development of a position on a given public issue? What candidates should a corporate political-action committee support—only those who are believed to have the company's best interests in mind and to share traditional business values? Shall corporate political strategies be judged solely on their short-term effectiveness—for example, in helping to defeat a certain bill that business does not like? Again, the nagging question of defining social betterment or, in a public-policy context, of defining the public interest, reappears.

Regarding the institutional context, there is the question of the role government should play in shaping business behavior. Should government continue with a command-and-control system of regulation to accomplish social objectives, or should it adopt other incentive mechanisms more consistent with market behavior? Can the market really be used to achieve social objectives? On the other side of the coin, what is the correct role of business in the political process? Lobbying activities, advocacy advertising, and particularly political-action committees represent potential time bombs for business. If business is perceived as too influential in the political process and too threatening to the pluralistic nature of American society and if its behavior is seen as too self-serving and not cognizant of the broader public interest, adverse public reaction can be expected.

And, finally, the absence of a clear moral foundation for public-policy involvement still presents a problem. The public-policy paradigm devotes most attention to events lying outside the firm in the political-governmental arena, paying less to the internal managerial skills and organizational modifications needed for an organization to attain a posture of social responsiveness and to the range of ethical and moral issues generated by the operation of business in today's world. Does the proactive approach, which is popular today, simply mean that business attempts to minimize the impact of social change on itself? Does not business have more obligation to society than is evident in self-serving attempts to manipulate the political environment? Does not business have a moral obligation that goes beyond obeying the law and complying with government regulations to consider the broader public interest? If business does have social and political responsibilities as well as economic ones, on what are they based? These difficult questions inspire a renewed interest in business ethics, corporate culture, and comparative normative systems.

PERSPECTIVES ON BUSINESS AND PUBLIC POLICY FROM POLITICAL ECONOMY

Gerald Keim

One way to approach the subject "business and public policy" is through the perspective of political economy. Courses in this area usually include broad topics: rationales for regulation of business activities, involving discussions of social control of business; descriptions of the nature and implementation of regulations pertaining to business activities; effects of regulations on impacted parties; business efforts to influence public-policy decisionmaking; and comparative discussion of the various formal and informal arrangements between business and government decisionmakers in different countries.

The business-and-public-policy area is interdisciplinary in scope, drawing on studies of: (1) markets and market failures; (2) industry structure, conduct, and performance; (3) firm structure and performance; (4) legislative structure, politics, and policy outcomes; (5) legal and regulatory structures, politics, and policy outcomes; and (6) cultural differences and their influences on decisionmakers in these various private- and public-sector settings. In addition to management research, theoretical and empirical material from political science, law, economics, sociology, and anthropology has been incorporated.

THE INDIVIDUALIST PERSPECTIVE

One useful contribution of modern political science and economics is the focus on the individual as the unit of analysis. In these disciplines, the representative individual is assumed to be motivated by his or her own self-interest. According to this perspective, it is more revealing not to view organizations (i.e., corporations, labor unions, interest groups, Congress, regulatory commissions, society) as decisionmaking units; instead, corporate executives and managers, elected public representatives, staffers and regulators, leaders of relevant organized interest groups and members, and individual citizens are considered the key actors. Personal values and ethics as well as organizational incentives and constraints will affect the behavior of individuals. For the purposes of this discussion, we will assume that values and ethics are randomly distributed across the set of individual actors. This is not to say that personal values and ethics are not important behavioral factors; however, we exclude them temporarily from consideration to permit examination of institutional or organizational influences on the incentives and constraints encountered by individual actors.

For illustrative purposes, this perspective may be contrasted with one that ignores the incentives confronting individual players. The so-called public-interest model of legislative behavior assumes that elected officials will attempt to serve the public interest and does not explicitly consider the incentives or constraints that may encourage or hinder an individual legislator's pursuit of such a goal. As an example, legislators' preoccupation with short-run effects of proposed legislation is sometimes considered to be evidence of having elected "bad" legislators. However, contemporary political scientists recognize that the length of the elected term and the amount of political information possessed by individual voters and interest groups often encourage (some would say force) legislators to maintain such a perspective. Thus, replacing "bad" legislators with "good" ones might have little effect on this temporal bias as long as the term of office and the level of information among voters remain unchanged.

Social Control of Business and Incentives of Individual Actors

The individualist perspective is also useful in uncovering a conceptual asymmetry that some management scholars have incorporated in their discussions of public and private institutions. Proponents of increased "social control" of corporations argue that self-interested managers and executives will pursue economic (profit) goals at the expense of other social considerations, such as environmental pollution, workplace or product safety, community reactions to plant closings, etc. According to this logic, the behavior of self-interested corporate decisionmakers requires more control than is usually found in the marketplace. Often the advocated form of social control is increased government regulation, new legislation, or the addition of outside members to a firm's board of directors. However, this viewpoint should also take into account the self-interest of those expected to exercise social control, whether they be regulators, legislators or board members. What will make these individuals less preoccupied with their own interests and more attentive to social concerns? That is, what incentives and feedback mechanisms will encourage these individuals to do a better job of responding to social concerns than corporate executives do?

Public-opinion polls suggest that many individual citizens do not have much confidence that elected or appointed officials will pursue the public interest, however it is defined. How can this observation be reconciled to proposals for increased social control? It is as if those advocating such an increase see self-interest as the primary motivating force only for individuals in the private sector. Regulators, legislators, and outside board members are, at least implicitly, expected to serve the public interest selflessly by exercising the appropriate social control over corporate decisionmakers. If this were true, would it not be possible to internalize the function in corporations by replacing current executives with regulators, legislators, and other more altruistic executives from the public sector?

A more symmetric analysis of decisionmakers in business and government views both sets as self-interested actors. Consideration of the incentives and constraints likely to influence both the public and private sectors is necessary to understand the possible effects of policy changes such as increased social control of corporations. This is also the case with proposals for government-business partnerships in the area of national industrial planning. Specific attention must be paid to the benefits for the public and private members of the partnership to determine what the end result of such cooperation is likely to be.

NORMATIVE VERSUS MORE OBJECTIVE PERSPECTIVES

One way to classify investigations in business and public policy is to array them on a spectrum ranging from more to less normative. The more normative research questions are motivated by a desire to find "correct" solutions to problems according to some set of values. The less normative research questions take the form of "what is occurring?" or "what would happen if institutional arrangements changed?" One could argue that it is prudent for the less normative work to come first. For example, it would seem that inquiries to determine if there is indeed a causal relationship between board structure in large corporations and the social performance of firms should precede research to determine the ideal board structure to promote corporate social responsibility in large firms.

Attempting to differentiate research perspectives in this manner leads to the consideration of another fundamental conceptual issue. Some scholars in the business-and-public-policy area commit their energies to solving social problems. But what is the definition of a social problem? Interestingly, there is little discussion in the area's literature devoted to developing a generic definition of these problems. Yet there is no shortage of articles on the problems of pollution, plant relocation, discrimination in the workplace, workplace or product safety, etc.

In our literature, either explicitly or implicitly, social problems seem to occur when some individual or individuals prefer(s) another outcome or situation to that which presently exists. Changing outcomes is costly, and this is usually at least part of the reason change has not occurred. It appears that analysis of the incremental costs and benefits of making changes should be an important part of our research literature.

The 1984 Union Carbide accident in Bhopal, India, may be used as an example. Presumably the risk of unintended release of large quantities of toxic substances could have been diminished by the company, with an attendant decrease in the probability of deaths from such an accident. What would have been the prospective costs and benefits of various incremental changes to reduce the risk of accidents of this type? That is, was the firm at the appropriate margin or would the prospective costs of incremental reductions in risk have generated benefits net of costs at the margin? Other relevant questions here might include whether the insurance and liability markets were efficient or whether a market failure prevented the firm from bearing the liability of such accidents. The mere observation that such an accident occurred tells us little about the appropriate prospective behavior of the firm. It is at least conceivable that the safety standards would be considered too strict if the value of forgone fertilizer production from plants with higher operating costs (or plants choosing not to locate in India at all) were greater on the margin than the expected reduction in risk of death or injury. Simply put, this logic reminds us that, from the perspective of the members of a community, state, or nation, the optimal level of most social "bads" is not zero if the incremental reduction of existing bads is too costly. This insight is a central contribution resulting from the integration of the political-economy perspective into research, theory, and teaching in business and public policy.

MANAGEMENT USES OF BUSINESS AND SOCIETY

George C. Sawyer

When business and society came to be developed, mainly in the 1960s, the driving force was the need to understand the social responsibility of business. Business leaders had to be persuaded to operate in a better way, and students had to learn how a socially responsible business should be managed. But responsible behavior was hard to define, and the cure to business/society problems turned out not to be as simple as persuading business leaders to behave responsibly. Responsibility, like a moral code, had an inward focus on the ethics of management actions, but the problems were out in society. These problems were poorly understood, multiplying rapidly, and demanding definition before any sort of code could be applied to their solution. At this point, the standards shifted a bit—it was now thought more important for business leaders to manage responsively, with prompt reaction to society's problems and needs.

But economic and political pressures also entered strongly into the equation, and society's rulemaking powers were found both to help and to hinder the search for a responsive or responsible management process. With its rapid growth, government itself entered the business/society equation, emerging as a third factor, with its purchases, its regulations, its own expectations of business. Government is controlled by society, but often only remotely, as it enforces its rules and pursues its purposes in an almost semiautonomous fashion.

This business/government/society triad was recognized by the addition of the middle element to the business-and-society course content and in the names of texts and courses. Society has a theoretical, ultimate power, but government is a separate major force in the social control of business. In order to operate, a business must live by whatever laws and government exist, right or wrong, or have those controls changed.

Some past failures of business responsibility are now seen as resulting from the absence of a needed regulation or law, such as the Clean Waters Act, or from badly conceived economic incentives, such as excessive tax concessions to oil companies. The general intent becomes more and more to achieve the optimum development of society through some equilibrium between the evolution of responsible or responsive business behavior and government incentives and controls.

DEVELOPMENT OF THE PUBLIC POLICY FOCUS

Recognition of the government role is causing the business-and-society field to mature into two related and compatible emphases, the traditional handling the education of those who will be business managers or otherwise will participate in the business process and a newer area dealing with improved formulation of public policy in order that the role of government in a modern society may be better discharged.

The public-policy direction is important, as is shown by the creation of numerous degree programs and schools focusing on public policy and its formulation. It is highly appropriate that a part of such a program be an effective presentation of this business/government/society relationship with a view to helping students understand the role of government and the ways it can be modified to serve society's interests more surely and more efficiently.

NEW CHALLENGES TO BUSINESS MANAGEMENT

The business-management direction is an equally important aspect of the continued evolution of business schools for the training of future managers and specialists. Managers need to understand how the operation of a firm affects society and how its impacts can be managed. Managers must also learn how a business must participate in public processes, including regulation, in order to function successfully in the modern world.

But the public demands on business management are taking a new direction with a new urgency. Where the first call for social responsibility emphasized moral behavior and the ethics of managing properly, now society is focusing instead on the results of the process. And where initially the request for responsive management was accompanied by a generally positive attitude toward the chances of curing society's problems, society is now beginning to insist that such problems be prevented altogether.

The Union Carbide tragedy at Bhopal in 1984 provides an illustration of how current public opinion can hold a corporation responsible for failing to anticipate a potential for injury to employees and public. The heavier burden on business management will be based on the fact that, in its role as change agent and creator of new products and services, the business firm continually deals in areas new to the regulators and therefore has the primary role in avoiding risk to the public.

This is a return to the original concept of business social responsibility, but with a new thrust. Neither social responsibility nor social responsiveness is sufficient. The key is prevention—good intentions or moral actions are no substitute. Responsiveness is a good way to solve problems, but why should management allow serious problems to occur at all? A business is now expected to anticipate and manage its social impacts. The management of social impact can be used as an effective guide for a management expected to operate both profitably and to the benefit of society. There are other approaches, but the evolving requirement is for a standard of performance for business operation that causes fewer problems for society than would otherwise be the case. This standard has been growing in the public consciousness in recent years, and the Bhopal tragedy seems to have hurried its development significantly. Over the next few years, study of business environment will need to afford more and more recognition to this standard.

The recent evolution of the business-environment course content, therefore, is toward a separation between those concerns that are more closely related to public-policy training and those elements that fit more into the general practice of management. Yet, business managers will always need an understanding of the public-policy processes from which changes in laws and regulations arise, while public-policy managers must understand the nature of business and the constraints within which it must operate. Thus, although each of these two streams of theory, research, and corporate action has its own inherent vitality and purpose, each complements and reinforces the other.

CHAPTER 4

The International Dimension in Business Environment

David J. Fritzsche and Steven L. Wartick

Internationalizing the business curriculum has been a widely discussed topic since 1974, when the AACSB incorporated "the international dimension of business operations" into its common body of study. The AACSB was merely formalizing a development that most practitioners and students of business had already recognized—the international dimension of business, especially in the post-World War II period, had become one of the most important factors in both business practice and business study.

In the field of business environment, the AACSB change was more gradual than dramatic. Formal development of the field had begun in the early 1960s, and scholars had quite naturally included the international dimension in this relatively new area of business study. In the business-and-society courses of that time, the question was never whether nor how to incorporate the international dimension; rather, the continuing concern was what from the mass of international business and societal interactions should be covered.

AN HISTORICAL PERSPECTIVE

The development of an international dimension within business environment has been primarily influenced by two factors. First, the field moved from a heavy macro orientation to a more balanced macro/micro orientation; treatment of the international dimension followed this shift. Second, with the concurrent development of the international business (IB) field itself, international topics in business environment became more well defined. Each of these factors deserves more detailed discussion.

Increasing Balance Within Business

The emphasis in the early texts and writings in business and society is heavily institutional, that is, macro oriented. Eells and Walton (1962) examined the "conceptual foundations of business." McGuire (1963) discussed interinstitutional relationships—labor/management relations, business and the media, etc. The first edition of Davis and Blomstrom (1966) worked from a strong societal emphasis. All these early works on the relationship between business and society stressed business as an institution within a societal setting.

Into these works, most discussions of the international dimension start by identifying the multinational corporation (MNC) as a change agent in host-country affairs. Cultural and political adjustments are mentioned, yet the emphasis is mainly on macroeconomic effects, such as balance-of-payments changes, trade protection, economic development, and direct foreign investment. Thus, like most early business-and-society study, consideration of the international dimension remained on the macro level of generalization and analysis.

Beginning in the late 1960s and continuing to the present, business environment has incorporated more of a microeconomic perspective. The macro, or institutional, orientation remains, yet increasing attention is given to organizational matters, reflected in the development of social responsibility, social responsiveness, and issues management in the business-and-society area (Wartick and Cochran 1985). The change to a more balanced orientation is also evident in the manner in which scholars in business environment have dealt with such issues as pollution, equal employment opportunity, and consumerism. The organizational responses to these environmental uncertainties, as well as the institutional, are now addressed in business environment. As an overarching element, business ethics has also become important. By the mid-1970s, Preston (1975) had summarized its evolution, distinguishing its three main perspectives as institutional, organizational, and philosophical.

Again, the international dimension remained consistent with the overall development of the field. Events such as the increased disclosure of foreign payoffs and bribes, the marketing of infant formula in developing countries, and the growing controversy over apartheid in South Africa led business-environment scholars to the examination of MNC responses to issues in other countries. Codes of conduct, corporate governance, public-policy effects, and ethical implications of organizational actions in the international arena became topics of serious attention. Study of the international dimension thus became more balanced between macro and micro concerns, as well as more relevant to individual managers and to corporations engaged in international business.

The Development of International Business

As the field of international business matured, the effects on the international dimension of business environment were significant. In some schools, separate IB courses were created, and the international material covered in business environment was proportionately decreased. If an IB course were required in the core, then the international dimension of business environment was treated even more selectively. Macro concerns generally covered in the required IB course (e.g., balance of payments, direct foreign investment, economic development, and cultural differences) appeared as mere background factors in the more specific international topics considered in business environment. Study of micro concerns (e.g., codes of conduct, ethical dimensions, and public policy analysis) was limited to the aspects relevant to given business-environment issues or problems, such as payoffs and bribes. In general, as specific IB courses were added to the curricula of business schools, the scope of the international dimension in business environment became more precise.

At schools where specific IB courses were not offered, the curriculum was internationalized through the inclusion of more of the international dimension in the core courses. Interestingly, the effect on business environment was again a refinement rather than an expansion of relevant international topics. Before the AACSB emphasis on internationalizing the curriculum, business environment was often the curricular home for IB material. As marketing, finance, policy, accounting, and management courses incorporated international concerns, business-environment courses could cover less breadth of international topics, adopting instead a more defined view of specific issues and key elements (e.g., business ethics) in the international dimension.

Most studies suggest that no clear consensus has developed about whether internationalizing the business curriculum should rest on developing new IB courses or on including IB material in existing courses (Task Force on Business and International Education 1977; Grosse and Perritt 1980). As far as business environment is concerned, the effect is the same under either approach. As the IB field has broadened, the international dimension in business environment has become more refined.

THE CURRENT SITUATION

To examine the current status of the international dimension of business environment, we have considered three sources of information. Papers presented from 1978 to 1984 at the Social Issues in Management Division of the Academy of Management reflect recent research. The body of texts released in the mid-1980s, specifically 1984–85, indicates to what degree the international dimension has become an established component of business environment. A series of interviews with fourteen professors who currently teach a general graduate or undergraduate business-and-society courses[1] addresses pedagogy, materials, and the question of change.

SIM Division Papers

From 1978 to 1984, nineteen papers relating specifically to the international dimension of business environment were presented at the SIM (Social Issues in Management) Division of the Academy of Management. These papers represent three general types of studies—comparative, issue, and country. The following listing shows the breadth of topics covered:

I. Comparative Studies

    A. "Business Response to Social Conflict: A Comparative Analysis" (Sethi 1977).

    B. "Social Performance Goals in the Peruvian and Yugoslav Worker Participation System" (Hoover, Troub, Whitehead, and Flores 1978).

    C. "The U.K. and European Experience" (MacMillan 1978).

D. "Corporate Responsibility and the Market Ethos: A Comparison of Great Britain and the United States" (Vogel 1982).

E. "A European Perspective on Business and Public Policy" (Dierkes 1982).

F. "A Comparison of the Ethical Behavior of American and German Managers" (Fritzsche and Becker 1983).

G. "Business Ethics: A Cross-Cultural Comparison of Managers' Attitudes" (Fritzsche and Becker 1984).

H. "European Co-determination" (Meek 1984).

II. Issue Studies

A. "Marketing of Infant Formula Food in Less Developed Countries: Some Public Consequences of Private Action" (Sethi and Post 1978).

B. "Labor Market Problems of the Disadvantaged Workers: An Analysis of Approaches" (Jain 1978).

C. "An Exploration of Remedies for Bribery in Foreign Markets" (Johnson 1981).

D. "A Brief Dissection of Bribery in Foreign Markets" (Johnson 1982).

E. "Who Should Control the Nationalized Company?" (Walters 1982).

F. "Institutionalizing Corporate Social Responsiveness: Lessons Learned From Eight Years of Experimentation" (Dierkes and Antal 1984).

G. "A Re-examination of Relationships Between Business Self-Interest, Wealth Creation and Community Well-Being (MacMillan 1984).

III. Country Studies

A. "Social Performance Goals in the Peruvian and Yugoslav Worker Participation System" (Hoover, Troub, Whitehead, and Flores 1978).

B. "Social Performance in German Industry" (Dierkes 1978).

C. "Corporate and Public Policy in France" (Rey 1978).

D. "Current Issues in the Canadian Business Environment" (Schroeder, Sexty, LeCasse, and Pasquero 1982).

E. "Ethical Dilemmas of Public Sector Executives in a Developing Economy" (Ajuogu 1982).

    F. "Developments in Industrial Democracy in Australia" (Volard 1983).

    G. "Public Policy and Technological Innovation in Swedish Banking" (King 1984).

    H. "The Politics of Protection, Expansion and Escape: International Collaboration and Business Power in U.S. Foreign Trade Policy" (Lenway 1984).

The papers can also be categorized according to Preston's three major perspectives of business and society (1975). Six of the papers (IA, IB, IIA, IIF, IIIA, and IIIC) relate to corporate social performance—the organizational perspective; eight (IC, IF, IIB, IID, IIIB, IIIE, IIIF, and IIIG) address business and public policy—the institutional perspective; five ID, IE, IIC, IIE, and IIID) deal with business ethics—the philosophical perspective. These papers represent the leading edge of research on the international dimension of business environment.

Recent Texts

Whereas papers at the SIM Division reflect newer ideas, topics in more recent textbooks fall into the established areas generally included in the study of the international dimension of business environment. A review of three of these recent texts—Aram (1983), Davis and Frederick (1984), and Steiner and Steiner (1985)—suggests that international questions are frequently examined through the triangular relationship of the multinational corporation (MNC), host-country demands, and home-country demands. Within this three-way context, any number of issues may be analyzed. For example, the issues of foreign payoffs and bribes, apartheid in South Africa, nationalization of corporate assets, appropriate technology, acid rain, and marketing infant formula are routinely discussed in business-environment texts by means of this relationship. MNCs are in many cases considered to be caught between the conflicting social, political, economic, and technological demands of home and host societies. The organizational analysis and response to these conflicts now seem to attract increasing attention. Interconnection and cultural relativity are strongly stressed.

1985 Interviews

During February and March of 1985, telephone interviews were conducted with fourteen professors who currently teach in business environment. The interviews were fairly informal, intended to solicit only general comments about the present status of the international dimension. The respondents were asked to address three general concerns: (1) how the international dimension is integrated into their business-environment courses; (2) what materials are most useful and what materials are still needed; and (3) whether they are satisfied with the current treatment of the international dimension in business environment.

Responses to the first question ranged from the observation that the international dimension was "rather thinly" covered to the belief that it was being fully integrated into all topics. However, most of those interviewed reported that one or two weeks are set aside to consider the international dimension specifically, and other international topics are discussed when appropriate as peripheral matters or extensions of the basic business-environment concepts. One respondent suggested that the international component is best placed at the end of the course because its study calls for an integration of all of the major business-environment theories and perspectives, yet opinions about the content of such study also varied substantially. Some suggested that international issues and currently relevant topics should be covered. Others said that specific issues are not important; rather, the emphasis should be on analyzing the social impact of the multinational corporation or the interrelatedness of the demands placed on the MNC. In this approach, issues may be used to illustrate the conceptual framework or the complexity of the international dimension, but are not considered sufficient by themselves. Respondents frequently used the terms "comparative approaches" and "relativism." General interests in corporate social performance, business and public policy, and ethics were also cited.

Regarding the second query, cases were overwhelmingly suggested as the major tool. Of particular importance were those relating to marketing infant formula, questionable foreign payments, and apartheid in South Africa, although others such as Dresser Industries and Union Carbide in Bhopal were also noted. As would be expected, cases were combined with other materials—journal articles, newspapers, monographs, films, and lectures—in an attempt to provide a more complete view of the international dimension. Yet, cases were by far the most frequently mentioned.

A few respondents felt that some important topics (e.g., industrial policy, the Foreign Corrupt Practices Act, counterfeiting products, and trade restraints) cannot be adequately addressed through cases. In these instances, they said, articles must be relied on more heavily. Yet there was general dissatisfaction with existing articles, centered around two major voids in the literature: There is no descriptive history of the evolution of MNCs and their interactions with governments and multiple cultures, and no broader theoretical frameworks are available that incorporate and describe alternative (including radical) social, political, and economic thinking. Some suggested that such organizations as the Interfaith Center for Corporate Responsibility, the Investor Responsibility Research Center, and the United Nations were useful sources of information. Others mentioned a few articles that start to address the voids but fall short of providing thorough analyses. In the main, however, the development of the international dimension in the literature of business environment was considered to be lacking.

From the preceding, it should not be surprising that almost all of the respondents believed that the current treatment of the international dimension in business environment could be improved. In general, the respondents recognized that the international dimension is continuing to increase in importance and that teaching and research should reflect this trend. Yet, there was concern about balancing the international dimension and the more traditional domestic view. A body of knowledge about international business and society may develop, but that material may be too much for one course. In sum, there was an overall perception of the need to expand the international dimension, but the precise scope of this expansion was not so apparent.

It is worth noting that three of the topical issues most frequently discussed both in the scholarly literature of the field and in courses concern international questions: the Nestle infant-formula issue; Union Carbide in Bhopal, India, and apartheid in South Africa. In each case, the conflict between cultural norms and expectations, the gap in the material circumstances of life between the developed and the less developed countries, and the ambiguities of international law and codes of conduct are integral aspects of the situation. In each case, there is international mobilization of public opinion and political pressure. Use of the business-environment and business-ethics framework appears to have particular merit in these types of problems.

THE CENTRALITY OF INTERRELATEDNESS

Even in the general business-environment course, the international dimension must be addressed to a certain degree. But analysis of the international level in business environment prompts considerations that are ignored in the domestic treatments of both the business-and-society area and other business-school courses. Complexity grows as conflicting cultural and political demands are placed on the MNC. Diversity increases as alternative ways of thinking about the role of business and society are proposed. As both interviews and recent texts have revealed, emphasis on interrelatedness is key when the study of business and society moves to the study of business and *societies.* It is a basic element in any discussion of the international dimension. Corporate social performance, business and public policy, and business ethics stand as the general perspectives of business and society, but the interaction and reciprocal impact of MNC decisions on multiple social and political structures become the central concept. "When in Rome . . . " may be an acceptable criterion for judging interaction between business and society on the national level. But when implications involve home-country sociopolitical structures and values or host-country structures and values, understanding of interrelatedness is paramount. In short, the number and nature of corporate stakeholders change as business-environment issues move to the international level. Central lessons come from analyzing the competing demands of these corporate stakeholders and the alternative means to address their needs.

How interrelatedness within the international dimension may be integrated into business-environment courses is constrained by at least two factors—availability of materials and the individual style of the instructor. For example, cases have probably become so popular as the vehicle for exploring the international dimension because they allow close examination of complex interactions. But they are also seen as the best available tool for teaching the international dimension because of the perceived lack of alternatives. As other materials become available, cases may be used less. The point is that availability of materials at least partially determines how the international dimension can be taught.

Instructor style is best illustrated by examples where the international component is included in the course. As suggested by the interview respondents, the international dimension can be a segment of business environment or it can be a continuing theme running through various courses. Given different backgrounds of instructors, availability of material, and class objectives, either approach seems workable. The choice depends on instructor preferences and teaching styles.

In conclusion, how the international dimension is incorporated into business-and-society courses seems less important than assuring that the increased complexity of interrelated stakeholder demands is somehow addressed. To elucidate this core concept, particular issues, cases, and articles may be used. New theoretical frameworks and integrative models may be developed. New materials that fill the voids in the business-environment literature may be offered. But, increasingly, emphasizing the international dimension seems to be one of the primary tasks for those who study and teach business and society.

For management as a whole, no challenge is so pressing as the new competitiveness and international linkages of the global economy. Management theory and research must develop a more adequate treatment of international business for it to retain its relevance in coming decades. The business-environment and business-ethics traditions are uniquely positioned and equipped to make substantial contributions in this area.

NOTE

1. The following respondents were included in the protocol: Steven N. Brenner, Portland State University; Rogene A. Buchholz, University of Texas at Dallas; Edwin M. Epstein, University of California, Berkeley; John E. Fleming, University of Southern California; R. Edward Freeman, University of Minnesota; Kirk O. Hanson, Stanford University; Robert E. Hogner, Florida International University; Thomas M. Jones, University of Washington; Gerald Keim, Texas A&M University; Karen Paul, Rochester Institute of Technology; Lee E. Preston, University of Maryland; John F. Steiner, California State University, Los Angeles; Richard E. Wokutch, Virginia Polytechnic Institute and State University; and Donna J. Wood, University of Pittsburgh.

CHAPTER 5

Ethics and Values in Management Thought

Otto A. Bremer, John E. Logan,
and Richard E. Wokutch

HISTORICAL OVERVIEW

The position of ethics and values in management thought has been and continues to be the subject of considerable debate. On the one hand, a strong tradition within the field asserts that ethics and values are an integral part of all issues, topics, and courses within the business-environment or business-and-society field. On the other hand, there is a vigorous movement to isolate the study of ethics and values as an academic discipline derived mainly from a philosophical orientation. Indeed, as business ethics comes to be treated in more and more areas of the curriculum and more and more courses, not only in business environment but also in the functional areas of business, a trivialization of the subject could result, if important conceptual and theoretical distinctions are glossed over in favor of specific applications. Sometimes the prevailing culture of the business school demands an overly pragmatic approach, emphasizing managerial practices and strategies and crowding out thorough discussion of ethical traditions. Too, the current renaissance of interest in corporate culture, which concentrates on the study of more theoretical areas—such as ethics and values—within the business curriculum, can at the same time define those areas purely in terms of pragmatic or sociological concepts rather than philosophical or moral ones.

We may identify three waves of discussion of business ethics in this century. A large number of texts on business ethics were produced by the first wave, during the 1920s and 1930s as indicated by Dean Wallace Donham's *Harvard Business Review* article, "Some Recent Books on Business Ethics" (1927). These discussions were extremely pragmatic and issue oriented. *Policy and Ethics in Business* (Taeusch 1931) was representative of the emphasis of the time. An early chapter on religious and social ideas discussed the role of religious ideologies in shaping business actions. The main content, however, consisted of more than 300 pages devoted to the Sherman Antitrust Act, pricing, the FTC, and the Clayton Act. A final section on self-regulation credited laws and regulations with generating an awareness of the need for self-governance in business. Also typical is an early book by two University of Wisconsin professors, entitled *Business Ethics* (Sharp and Fox 1937). It contained chapters on advertising practices, service, deception, and other ethical issues. Among the section headings in the book were "Fair Service," "Fair Treatment of Competitors," and "Moral Progress in the Business World." The topical treatment was much narrower than would be characteristic of a business-ethics text today.

The second wave of interest in business ethics came in the 1950s and 1960s. A substantial number of the textbooks and casebooks in this period were the work of scholars at Catholic universities, such as Loyola University of Chicago, the University of Scranton, the University of Detroit, Marquette University and the University of Notre Dame. Many of these covered topics also addressed in the early business-and-society texts. In fact, during this interval, the terms "business ethics" and "corporate responsibility" tended to be used interchangeably. However, the ethics texts focused more heavily on individual behavior, whereas business and society texts usually stressed the impact of environmental variables on the business firm and executive decisionmaking. National church groups such as the Federal Council of Churches, the organizational predecessor of the National Council of Churches, began devoting attention to issues of ethics and values in business. The National Council of Churches' Department of Church and Economic Life published a significant series of monographs, including volumes by Boulding (1953) and Bunting (1953), as well as a summary work, *Ethics in a Business Society* (Childs and Cater 1954).

Baumhart's classic survey of *Harvard Business Review* readers regarding ethical attitudes and business practices (1961) received considerable attention in business-ethics texts. A typical text (Garrett 1963) covered topics such as honesty, expense accounts, personality tests, businesses' control over public opinion, and waste. Casebooks also appeared. One by four Catholic university professors (Garrett et al. 1968) covered cases relating to hiring, firing, and promotions, industrial relations, production, pricing, advertising, and government and community relations. Note again that the topical coverage tended to be narrower than in most texts of the 1980s.

While considerable business-ethics materials were being developed in the 1950s and 1960s, there were few business-ethics courses being taught in collegiate schools of business. In a 1953 survey of 100 universities and colleges, Bunting (1953) noted that 94 percent of these institutions did not offer business-ethics courses and that 75 percent of the respondents said that business ethics was treated in other courses. Luther Hodges, Secretary of Commerce under President Kennedy, noted in 1963 that few business schools offered business-ethics courses and that philosophy courses in ethics dealt with business ethics only incidentally. He argued that business-ethics seminars should be offered, particularly at the graduate level (Hodges 1963).

The third and current wave of attention to business ethics started in the 1970s. In the aftermath of Watergate and the foreign payoff scandals involving American firms, interest in ethics in general and business ethics in particular soared. At this time, business schools were growing rapidly and experiencing faculty shortages, while some liberal-arts colleges and liberal-arts departments in major universities were experiencing declining enrollment. One result of these events was that philosophy departments and faculty members become increasingly interested in developing and offering business-ethics courses. The same was true to a lesser extent among religious-studies faculty.

Several studies trace the history of business-ethics courses. McMahon (1975) found that in recent years 40 percent of the business-administration programs he surveyed had courses concerned with socioeconomic (socioethical) issues and that approximately 20 percent of the programs had a required course in this area. McMahon does not distinguish between courses that focus primarily on business ethics, as opposed to those that focus on social issues.

During this third wave, business ethics has come to be included in the field of business environment. Indeed, Buchholz (1979) noted that business ethics was the second most common topic covered in business-environment/public-policy courses. Hoffman and Moore (1982) analyzed the business-ethics course offerings of 685 colleges and universities and found that 48 percent offer at least one business-ethics course. Over 80 percent of these courses had been developed since 1973. More than half of these courses had titles other than "Business Ethics," such as "Business and Society," and more (48 percent) were housed in philosophy and religion departments than in business departments (38 percent). AACSB-member business schools were slightly more likely to offer such courses in the business school than were nonmember institutions.

A recent study conducted by the Opinion Research Corporation for the Ethics Resource Center (1979) surveyed graduate business schools exclusively, specifically the deans of AACSB-accredited MBA programs. Two findings of this study are particularly interesting for our purposes. First, very few graduate schools offer a separate business-ethics course. Instead, it was asserted that this subject matter is covered in other courses, especially business-and-society courses. Second, the responding deans overwhelmingly indicated that they felt that cases were the most important teaching material in this field.

Powers and Vogel (1980) remarked that the development of the field had been slowed both by the low volume of ethics teaching and uncertainty about the unifying theme, course content, and teaching methods. Business ethics, like the whole of the business-environment or business-and-society field, is multiparadigmatic, interdisciplinary in tradition, and eclectic in the types of scholars and scholarship appropriate to the area. However, the links between the business community and the academic community are alive and well in business ethics. Boundary-spanning organizations, such as the Center for Ethics and Social Policy at Berkeley, the Trinity Center for Ethics and Corporate Policy at Trinity Church of Wall Street, the Center for Ethics and Corporate Policy at Grace Episcopal Church in Chicago, the Forum for Corporate Responsibility in New York City, the Institute for Servant Leadership at Emory University, and the Ethnics Resource Center in Washington, D.C., contribute heavily to the ongoing vitality of the field.

DEFINING THE FIELD OF BUSINESS ETHICS

The expansion of business ethics as a field within business environment has been very rapid in recent years. Collectively, those currently teaching in the field have a rich variety of academic preparation in both philosophy and religious studies, as well as in management, including a variety of subdisciplines such as marketing, organizational development, and business policy. At this time, there is no great haste to determine the single best disciplinary background for an instructor in business ethics. Each discipline and tradition brings a perspective that can enrich the total effort. At some point, it will be necessary to discuss the appropriateness of "Business Ethics" as the title for a course dealing more broadly with value issues within a business culture. Ordinarily, analysis of a field is begun by defining, according to universally accepted conventions, its key terms—in this case, "ethics," "values," "morality," "good," "right," etc. In a pluralistic society, no universally accepted definitions of these terms exist. Yet the pragmatism of situation ethics carried to its extreme would in many ways contradict the very attempt to deal constructively with business-ethics issues, and so it would seem essential to arrive at some kind of consensus regarding the meaning of these concepts.

The variety of perspectives is very broad. For example, Davis and Frederick define ethics as "the rules or principles that define right and wrong" (1984: 76). Others say that "ethics in the broadest sense provides the basic conditions of acceptance for any activity" (Henderson 1982: 37) or simply "it is what I think is right." "What a person asserts is right or wrong is what a person making the statement thinks is good or bad" (Moore 1903: 4). Regarding values, Davis and Frederick quite precisely define them as "fundamental and enduring beliefs about the most desirable conditions and purposes of life" (1984: 74). Cavanagh is more instrumental, describing values as the "criteria upon which important decisions are made" (Cavanagh 1984: 1). Arrow is more personal, stating that "no sharp line can be drawn between taste and values" (Arrow 1951). Although a theoretical distinction can be made between ethics and values (Paul 1981), these two concepts frequently overlap. Ethics may be defined quite broadly as involving moral judgment or reflection on the moral significance of human action (McCoy 1985). "Business ethics," then, refers to such reflection on decisions made within the context of economic activity and corporate management.

The variety of perspectives will also be apparent in the kinds of questions addressed and the approach taken to them. There is wide agreement on the importance of distinguishing two kinds of questions: the empirical (often, simply, "what is?") and the normative ("what ought to be?"). Once these two questions are answered in a specific business situation, two derivative questions emerge—how to get from what is to what ought to be and what is the motivation behind the question, that is, why ask it at all? Discussion of specific business cases may rush to determine the desired action without adequate attention to the other three kinds of questions. This may result from inadequate familiarity with or attention to the conceptual and theoretical framework of business ethics.

The tension among the disciplines teaching business ethics is apparent in the varied approaches to questions and issues. For some, an empirical method is quite obvious—facts are facts. It thus becomes possible to extrapolate moral duties, such as respect for persons, beneficence, and justice, from the essential facts of human nature. In pluralistic societies, however, these facts may be culturally derived from a variety of traditions. Current discussion of corporate culture has called attention to the need for a consensus on assumptions about human nature. Certainly, it is not easy to prove empirically that any single set of motivations and attitudes—for example, MacGregor's Theory X or Theory Y—is *the* operative factor in human nature.

However, a normative statement is quite different from an empirical statement. There is no effective verification procedure for normative statements, which tell us what ought to be, not what is. We cannot say for sure what value judgments are "true," although we can often agree on matters of value. There will be those who will argue that the answers to normative questions are rooted in the fundamental beliefs and assumptions about reality held by an individual or community and will fight any consensus based on tradition or social-survey answers to normative questions.

There is, however, a very strong argument that the really valid reason for teaching business ethics is to incorporate into a firm's decisionmaking the basic agreement, according to Western thought, regarding essential facts about human nature, fundamental human values, and moral duties. Newton has developed the following business-ethics teaching tables to facilitate classification of a variety of ethical frameworks, fundamental responsibilities, and duties of managers and of corporations (see Tables 5–1 through 5–5).

Table 5–1. Background: Ethical Orientations.

Theory	Good to Be Reached as a Consequence	Verification Procedure: How to Know What to Do and When It's Done
Consequentialist Theories		
Utilitarianism: Hedonism (Bentham)	Maximum pleasure for the greatest number.	Discerning what is pleasurable is innate in people. The criterion for pleasure maximized is the moments of pleasurable consciousness felt by those affected, and only asking them will determine what result has been achieved.
Utilitariansim (J.S. Mill)	Maximum utility (pleasure or any other good—virtue, education, achievement) for the greatest number.	Utility, which includes judgments of quality of pleasure and long-term enlightenment, is much more difficult to quantify.
Rule utilitarianism	Formation of, and obedience to, rules of general obedience that will produce the greatest good for the greatest number.	Rule utilitarianism requires two-step verification; the good act is one in obedience to rule; the rule must be utilitarian.
Intuitionism (G.E. Moore)	Goodness, a nonnatural universal quality intuitively recognizable.	Each person is intuitively able to recognize goodness and distinguish it from all natural properties.
Self-realizationism or Virtue (Aristotle, Abraham Maslow)	Achievement of full development of human nature.	Very difficult to say. Attainment is usually associated with culturally approved characteristics: virtue, happiness, and success.

(Table 5–1. continued overleaf)

Table 5–1. continued

Theory	Source of Obligation	Verification Procedure: How to Know What to Do and When It's Done
Non-consequentialist Theories		
Law-based theories: Natural Law Theory (Aquinas)	Eternal Law of God.	That portion of God's law that is necessary for the moral life is immediately known to reason, engraved on the heart.
Formalism (Kant)	Nature of morality itself; moral law.	Act so that the reason for your act is generalizable to all moral agents (first formulation of the Categorical Imperative).
Rights-based theories: (Hobbes and Locke; Nozick)	The inalienable rights that persons have by nature, that others must respect.	Each person deserves at least to be regarded as a person, entailing at least the right to be free (to be left alone) and to be regarded as equal to other persons. Other rights (like property) are derived from liberty or equality or established by contract (see below).
Contract-based theories: (Hobbes and Locke; Rousseau, Rawls)	Agreements made by the agent (explicitly or tacitly).	Obviously, all contracts (or promises) explicitly undertaken create moral obligations. Beyond that, the conventions that make society possible are "tacitly" agreed to by all who accept the benefits of those conventions.

| Principle-based theories: (Ross, Fletcher; et al.) | A variety of moral principles (gratitude, honesty, compassion, etc.) that are *prima facie* binding on all agents. | These principles are intuitively known and need no external warrant. They occasionally conflict, which is why they do not bind absolutely. Reflection must determine which principle takes precedence in a given situation. |

Note: "Egoism," a purported form of consequentialism in which the good sought is the happiness of the actor alone, contradicts itself at the first level of any analysis and is not therefore treated here as a valid theory.

Source: Lisa Newton, Fairfield University, Fairfield, Connecticut, 1985.

Table 5–2. Principles and Problems of the Major Ethical Orientations.

Orientation	*Principle*: the position of the person who adopts this orientation.	*Response*: the problems that a serious respondent might see in the principle.
Nonmoral Orientations: Since these orientations make no claim to take other persons into account, they have no claim on our attention, and a "response" would be inappropriate.		
Pure impulse	I follow no rules, I do just what I feel like when I feel like doing it.	(And what, really, is there to say?)
Egoism	I always follow the rule: Do what is best for my own interests now and in the long run. I just look out for Number One.	(*Suggestion*: When this person is around, you look out for Number One.)
Nonphilosophical Moral Orientations: These orientations include moral rules, but make no claim that the rules are based on reasoning. The basic response to all of them is that they should be subjected to rational examination, for they are terribly prone to error.		
Religion	I don't need to worry about right and wrong, because the Bible (or, the doctrine of my Church or revealed religion) tells me everything I need to know.	But how do you settle disputes between members of different churches or people who read the Bible differently? Not all true believers agree, you know.
Conscience (moral sense)	I just know what is right and wrong, and I do (or don't do) it. I let my conscience be my guide.	Sometimes, deep prejudices feel very much like the presentations of conscience. Are you sure you can never be mistaken?
Group consensus	I do what my group (team, company) expects me to do, just because it is my group, and it wants me to do it.	Whole groups have gone off the deep end at some points in history (witness Nazi Germany). If your whole group is wrong, you have a duty to break with it.

Ethical Orientations:

Natural law	There is an unchanging Law of Nature logically coherent and capable of being known through reflecting on man's universal and unchanging human nature. Basic principles are derived from this reflection on human nature, and they are said to be binding on all men and women of all times in the past, the present, and the future.	Despite careful reasoning by great philosophers, there remains substantial disagreement about what the Law says. It just is not as clear as you say it is.
Teleological (or Consequentialist) theories	Acts are right if they result in the greatest good for the greatest number in the long run. "Good" might mean "achievement of natural end" (Aristotle) or "happiness (pleasure)" (the Utilitarians: Jeremy Bentham and John Stuart Mill). In any situation, I try to do what will make as many people as possible as good or happy as possible.	On such a theory, you could violate the rights of small minorities quite terribly, and if a large majority was made better or happier by the injury, the theory would justify it. Are you sure you want to buy into this result?
Deontological theories	Acts are right if they are done out of duty, on the motive of conformity to the moral law (Categorical Imperative: Immanuel Kant) or moral imperatives that would apply to anyone in the same circumstances. I try to discover my duty by asking: what would happen if everyone acted as I plan to act?	Rigid adherence to "principles," no matter how moral, can result in really terrible injury to other human beings. The Categorical Imperative is only a formal principle; other considerations, probably teleological, are needed to make it useful.

(Table 5–2. continued overleaf)

Table 5-2. continued

Ethical Orientations: (continued)

Single-principle theories	Acts are wrong if they violate certain important principles: Social Justice (Rawls), Liberty (Nozick), and Love (Fletcher) are popular examples of such principles. I try to be aware of these principles when I act. (*Note*: John Rawls, *A Theory of Justice*; Robert Nozick, *Anarchy, State and Utopia*; Joseph Fletcher, *Situation Ethics*).	At best, these are partial theories. They will not help you select the appropriate rule of action for real circumstances. They only remind you of certain values in our society that the theories' authors feel have been neglected or not made clear in recent literature.
Intuitionism	You know, you can cite rules and calculate consequences all night, and those exercises might be very useful for me to prepare to make a moral decision. But, ultimately, I have to follow the one course that I just see as the right one for the situation. I have no right to do anything else.	But how can you justify a decision, once made, or advise others in moral dilemmas? Although this is a reasoned position, each decision can produce no reasoning behind it, beyond some "intuition" that you claim to to be seeing. I think you may be hallucinating.

Source: Lisa Newton, Fairfield University, Fairfield, Connecticut, 1982.

Table 5-3. Fundamental Duties.

	Beneficence—Promoting Human Welfare	Justice—Acknowledging Human Equality	Respect for Persons—Honoring Individual Freedom
Basic fact about human nature that grounds the duty	Humans are animals, with vulnerable bodies and urgent physical needs, capable of suffering.	Humans are social animals, who must live in communities and therefore must adopt social structures to maintain communities.	Humans are rational, free, able to make choices, foresee the consequences, and take responsibility.
Value realized in performance of duty	Human welfare, happiness.	Human equality.	Human dignity, autonomy.
Working-out of the duty in ethical theory	Best modern example is utilitarianism, from Jeremy Bentham and John Stuart Mill, who saw morality as that which produced the greatest happiness for the greatest number. Reasoning is consequential, aimed at results.	Best modern example is John Rawls' theory of Justice as "fairness," maintaining equality unless inequality helps everyone. Reasoning is deontological: morality derived from duty, not consequences.	Best modern example is Immanuel Kant's formalism, where morality is seen as the working-out of the Categorical Imperative. Reasoning is deontological.
Samples of implementation in business	Protecting safety of employees, maintaining pleasant working conditions, contributing funds to the local community.	Obedience to law, enforcing fair rules, nondiscrimination, no favoritism, giving credit where credit is due.	Respect for employee rights, treating employees as persons, not just as tools, respecting differences of opinion.

Source: Lisa Newton, Fairfield University, Fairfield, Connecticut, 1985.

Table 5-4. The Duties of Managers.

Duty	Implementation (for example)	Grounds: Legal, Moral, and Practical
Duties to Employees: The Internal Constituencies		
Respect for Rights		
Nondiscrimination in hiring	Affirmative-action program at all levels.	*Legal*: Broadly, the Constitution. *Then*: civil rights legislation and court decisions, labor laws, EEOC, use of federal contract requirement.
Reward for performance	Scrupulous adherence to contract, fair and thorough personnel records, incentives.	
Privacy	Personnel inquiries strictly job related; no polygraphs.	*Moral*: Respect for autonomy of persons, equality, individual dignity.
Participation in community, exercise of rights of citizen	Noninterference in noncompany-related political activity.	*Practical*: Attitude of respect is essential to foster integrity, initiative, and moral behavior in the employees.
Concern for welfare		
Safety	Constant concern for safety: education, regulations, enforcement.	*Legal*: Labor laws, OSHA, workmen's compensation, income security, and maintenance programs.
Health	Maintenance of medical, exercise facilities.	*Moral*: Love of neighbor, especially responsibility for those in your care.

Economic security	Job stability, generous retirement benefits.	
Personnel and professional growth	Reimbursement for education, in-service training.	*Practical:* Genuine concern, regularly manifested, is associated with increased productivity, lower absenteeism and fewer errors in work.
Community participation and recreation	Contribution to recreational and other community activities in which employees participate.	

Source: Lisa Newton, Fairfield University, Fairfield, Connecticut, 1985.

Table 5–5. The Duties of Corporations.

Duty	Implementation (for example)	Grounds: Legal, Moral, and Practical
	Duties to the Community: The External Constituencies	
Customers		
Product Safety	Maintain highest standards of quality control in design and manufacture.	*Legal*: Strict liability; negligence; implied warranty. Consumer-protection laws.
Truth in selling	Choose marketing media and messages carefully.	*Moral*: Avoid harm (customer welfare); avoid deception (customer autonomy).
		Practical: Shoddiness and dishonesty generally backfire on sales.
Local Community		
Economic stability	Do not close plant on which community depends.	*Legal*: Tax and zoning laws, local regulation.
		Moral: Duty to help neighbors.
Philanthropy	Support nonprofit enterprise.	*Practical*: Keep workers and their families happy.
Natural Environment		
Nonpollution	State-of-the-art scrubbing devices; monitoring beyond legal requirements.	*Legal*: DEP (direct regulation); superfund; user fees and taxes.
Safe disposal of waste	Continue research into recycling and neutralizing of harmful waste substances.	*Moral*: Obligation to protect health, to preserve nature for future generations.
		Practical: Good PR; easier to work in pleasant surroundings.

Third World

Questionable payments	Avoid all payments that distort market or deflect officials from their jobs.	*Legal*: FCPA; treaties, restrictions such as tariffs, quotas, or embargoes.
Marketing harmful substances	Follow same safety standards abroad as at home, even where law is more permissive.	*Moral*: Obligation to other nations to help them develop on their own, independent and unexploited. *Practical*: Violent change in regime can wipe out trading partners and investments.
Support of racist, corrupt, or oppressive regimes	At minimum: Abide by Sullivan Principles, U.S. law, and supply no instruments of oppression.	

Source: Lisa Newton, Fairfield University, Fairfield, Connecticut, 1985.

TWO DIMENSIONS TO THE FIELD

The field of business ethics often includes two sets of issues not clearly related to each other—"microethical" matters that presuppose the existence (and fundamental goodness) of the present business system and "macroethical" questions on the desirability or necessity of different sets of large-scale economic arrangements and the possibility of radical change.

At the micro level, we are dealing with what can be called managerial ethics—the ethics of the enterprise. How does one know what is fair and just and right within the context of a given institution? Through these questions, it is possible to deal with specific issues confronting managers and executives. This corresponds to an issues-management strategy and policy orientation that fits well in the typical business-school culture. The macro approach is quite different. Ethics at this level is still not discussed very much in the United States, and there are few courses dealing with the ethics of economics. Economic ethics courses are really courses in contemporary or comparative economic systems: Marxist, capitalist, socialist and other economic systems. When such courses are taught from an ethical perspective, questions of fairness, equity, access, etc. are asked about the system as a whole. In the past, the American trust in the laissez-faire market system to provide justice seemed to make these questions unnecessary. However, these concerns are alive and well in Europe, Latin America, and other centers of academic thought and theory. These issues become material, indeed vital, for business courses as international business grows in importance and the internationalization of the business-school curriculum proceeds. Indeed, the internationalization trend is now focusing attention on questions having to do with the fairness and justice of basic societal institutions in a way that complements and reinforces considerations of these issues in business ethics.

These micro and macro levels are rather difficult to reconcile. It is hard to discuss ethical responsibilities and challenges in terms of opportunities within a corporation's operations and at the same time talk about the legitimacy of what business is doing. Some of the macro level, of course, comes into business-environment courses. Efforts are being made to explore the managerial implications of differing political/economic worldviews (Paul and Barbato 1985).

Using ethical/normative models and theories to analyze managerial decisions makes business ethics relevant in the education of managers.

Pedagogically, it is difficult and dangerous to separate the micro and the macro. The challenge is to know how to present micro issues in such a way as to force a consideration of how they add up and what kind of economic structure is desirable. Alternatively, teaching can start from an economic framework and then provide a good basis for questions about how individual management decisions are affected by the kind of economic structure within which the decisionmaker functions.

IDEOLOGY AND CORPORATE CULTURE

Increased attention is being given to ideology and its legitimate role within the teaching, discussion, and application of business ethics. For example, Lodge, in *The New American Ideology* (1975), suggests two ideologies: the classical Adam Smith individualism and what Lodge calls communitarianism. This last emphasis places more on membership rights and community need than on private property and individual consumer preferences. From the perspective of an economist, Okun (1975) hypothesized that tradeoffs are constantly taking place between equality and efficiency as guiding ideologies. From a philosophical orientation, the debate between followers of Rawls (1971) and followers of Nozick (1974) revolves around a similar juxtaposition of an ideology stressing "fairness" and one based on "freedom."

Textbooks used in teaching business ethics treat ideology with varying degrees of sensitivity. Chatov defines ideology as the link between beliefs and actions (1973). Cavanagh also spends considerable time on ideology in American business. He defines values as the criteria by which important choices are made. Ideology becomes a "constellation of values that have been integrated into a fairly comprehensive, coherent and motivating statement of purpose" (Cavanagh 1983: 1).

One of the concerns with which business ethics must deal more than it has in the past is the proper, legitimate, healthy role of the ideologies integral to organizational cultures. For example, Drucker says that the job of managers is to support the reason for being of their institutions, *whatever* that reason happens to be (1980). Study of this issue is crucial in business ethics. It raises the question of who is actually deciding the purpose of the organization or, put another way, of the legitimacy of the distribution of power in organizations. Problems of challenge and dissent within the corporation become significant. Topics such as whistle-blowing can be covered, with the recognition that this form of protest represents a challenge, usually on ethical grounds, to the authority of those who are deciding what is going on in an organization. The current interest in Japanese management prompts increased consideration of the use of paternalism, propaganda, and ideology as mechanisms for social control of individuals.

The teaching of business ethics will be changed significantly if the present interest in identifying the basic assumptions that underpin a firm's corporate culture continues. Attention to the "excellent corporation" (Peters and Waterman 1982) has largely focused on the artifacts—behaviors and policies—of the corporation, although there is some awareness of the need to determine the values that can be inferred from and that influence the development of the artifacts. In understanding the organizational culture of a firm, however, the crucial area is the underlying assumptions that are operative. According to Schein (1984: 6), these taken-for-granted basic assumptions include:

1. The organization's relationship to its environment;
2. The nature of reality and truth;
3. The nature of human nature;
4. The nature of human activity; and
5. The nature of human relationships.

A corporation tends to develop an organizational impetus both for external adaptation and for internal integration. Thus, both personal and corporate ethical issues are important. Future business-ethics courses will have to be increasingly concerned with the beliefs held by members of a firm and the relation of those individual beliefs to the assumptions of the firm as a whole. Schein suggests that in order to have an effective corporate culture the firm must reach consensus on criteria

> for distribution of power and status—pecking order;
> for intimacy, friendship, and love—rules for the relationship of peers and sexes;
> for allocation of rewards and punishment—what is "heroic" and "sinful" and what leads to "excommunication"; and

for an ideology and "religion"—how to explain the unexplainable and uncontrollable.

It may now be time for courses in business ethics to take the role of beliefs and values much more seriously and to begin integrating discussion of these issues into the study of corporate culture.

INDIVIDUAL AND ORGANIZATIONAL ETHICS

The relationship between individual and organizational ethics is another long-standing question (Werhane 1985). What difference, if any, exists between these two areas? There are those who argue that only individuals are moral agents. On the other hand, the question was answered positively in "Can a Corporation have a Conscience?" (Goodpastor and Matthews 1982). The latter presentation is helpful because, while *organizational* ethics might be discussed in business ethics, there is still a lingering suspicion that organizations are somehow incapable of acting as moral agents. It may be, however, that certain organizational structures encourage ethical behavior while others do the opposite (Velasquez 1983). This issue, of course, must be considered in relation to the organizational culture within business firms. How an ethics course is taught and the extent to which organizations or individuals become the primary unit of analysis will greatly influence the approach to this issue.

ATTENTION TO THE DECISIONMAKER

Finally, interest seems to be growing in the people making decisions, rather than being limited to what should be decided. This is not new. Leadership literature has generally suggested building an organization around healthy individuals (Barnard 1938; Schmidt and Tannenbaum 1958). But this advice brings us to new questions. Who is going to define what healthy individuals are? Where do they come from? It has always been assumed they come from good families, good schools, churches, synagogues. It is certainly not the task of business schools or corporations to produce them. Or is it?

One suspects that behind much of the support for business-ethics courses is the unspoken assumption that students who take such courses will act more ethically than those who do not. This explains why interest in these courses increases after upheavals such as price-fixing, Watergate, foreign-payments, or political-contributions scandals. Media coverage of alleged unethical conduct—for example, Union Carbide in Bhopal, E. F. Hutton's admission of bank fraud, and General Dynamics' and General Electric's extraordinary charges for military supplies and equipment—leads to heightened public awareness and academic consideration of business ethics. However, few instructors are willing to admit that their interests revolve around topical issues. Course objectives typically refer to the more widely accepted, achievable, and enduring goal of helping students to understand ethical issues and the ethical content of business decisions.

The literature abounds with scholars asking what the purpose of business-ethics courses should be and what the effects of such courses are (Arlow and Ulrich 1985; Barach and Nicol 1980; Konrad 1978; Purcell 1972; Stevens 1983). These questions remain paramount. With the exception of some of the Roman Catholic business schools, there is little explicit attention to "character formation" (Hauerwas 1974, 1977, 1981). Our Western culture tends much more to consider decisionmaking a simply technical process and decisionmakers ethically neutral—moral castrati, as it were. The call for ethics of character should be taken seriously (Lebacqz 1985). As more decisions are made in new and unknown situations, fraught with ambiguity and complicated by technological innovation, the values and virtue of the decisionmaker become more important.

THE CONTENT OF BUSINESS ETHICS

Business-ethics courses vary greatly from school to school. Content depends on the relation of this course to other courses offered, the qualifications and interests of the faculty available at a given time, the perceived mission of the institution, and, most of all, whether courses are offered by philosophy or by management departments. However, graduate level or upper-division undergraduate courses dealing with questions of ethics and values in business management generally have some content in the following areas:

1. Kinds of questions and statements.
   Basic distinctions must be clear among the kinds of questions that can be asked and kinds of statements that can be made. Certainly the difference between descriptive and normative questions and their relation to the practical action questions should be ad-

dressed. Some will want to clarify that statements can be *formal*—definitions, or true by definition, like mathematical equations; *empirical*—statements of fact, like scientific claims (natural or social sciences); or *normative*—like value judgments.

2. How ethical decisions are made.

Courses will differ according to the amount of attention given to classical ethical concepts, to how religious insights can be involved in management decisions (Bremer 1981), or to psychological considerations such as stages of moral development (Kohlberg 1981) or cognitive-dissonance theory. One primary aim of the course should be to help students identify their own values and how they relate to management decisions.

3. Effect of organizations on ethical decisionmaking.

At times ethics courses isolate discussion of management decisions from the organizational content. The danger is twofold: the choice of action is reached by a conceptual application of theory to practice for the generic issue being discussed, and/or there is little consideration given to the influence of company ideology or corporate culture on the making or acceptability of the decision. A number of topics will encourage sensitivity to these issues—whistle-blowing, expense-account reporting, relations with minorities and women, and the way work affects family life.

4. Internal decisions.

How company values relate to the dignity of the individual, interest in the growth and development of persons, together with productivity, is mainly visible in the areas of employee relations and human-resource practices. Personnel policies and actions on hiring practices, compensation, performance appraisals, and career development, as well as health, disability, and child-care benefits, should be covered to some degree. The actual issue selected is not as important as using it to discuss issues like who participates in what decisions, encouragement of job enrichment, and prejudice against racial, ethnic, age, gender, or religious groups. Internal company decisions also deal with product choice, marketing strategy, organizational structures, financing, and other corporate activities that have an ethical dimension.

Ethical issues in corporate governance are a part of many subsections of the business-environment field. The ethical aspects of this important topic should be addressed somewhere in management education. The same considerations apply to the broad topic of accountability within business firms. Accountability, for what and to whom, can be studied at many levels—individuals, companies, and associations—and in many ways—social accounting (Seidler and Seidler 1975), social audit (Bauer and Fenn 1972) and media exposure (Corson and Steiner 1974). We repeat, the ethical dimensions of this subject need attention within the total education of managers. A course in business ethics need not attempt to include all such activities, but students should be reminded that topics covered do not exhaust ethical issues.

5. External Company Decisions.
   Distinctions between internal and external company decisions can be artificial because the categories do overlap. However, the effects of company actions on those outside the firm must be recognized. The degree to which a corporation has a social responsibility to various stakeholders may vary, but a central concern should be the way seemingly rational internal policies can often have unforeseen and undesirable consequences for society as a whole. Discussion of topics such as credit policies, investment decisions, political activity, philanthropy, and questionable payments at home and abroad can be the means to promote understanding of this issue.

MATERIALS IN BUSINESS ETHICS

Teaching materials for business ethics reflect the historical development of the field. A substantial body of literature has evolved over the years, which considers ethical issues in business from a variety of disciplinary perspectives, including philosophy, management, sociology, theology, and public policy, and from the viewpoint of business practitioners. However, texts specifically intended for business-ethics courses have only begun to appear in significant numbers in the last few years. This emergence of teaching material has coincided with and signalled the resurgence of business ethics as a recognized discipline. The recent start-up of two new journals, *Business and Professional Ethics* in 1981 and *The Journal of Business Ethics* in 1982, reflects the new importance of the field.

The year 1979 marked a turning point in the development of text materials in business ethics. Several important texts, including Beauchamp and Bowie (1979), Donaldson and Werhane (1979), and

Barry (1979), were published that year. Since then the number of business-ethics texts and other teaching materials has grown. A listing of teaching materials available in several categories is provided in Appendix 3. This is by no means an exhaustive list. More comprehensive bibliographies of books and articles are available from the University of Virginia (Jones 1982), Bentley College (Hoffman and Moore 1982) and Creighton University (Bond 1984).

In recent years, the business-ethics content in standard business-environment texts has been upgraded considerably. Recent reports by the National Commission on Excellence in Education sponsored by the U.S. Department of Education (1983) and the Carnegie Foundation (Boyer 1987) have catalyzed the integration of ethical and moral issues into higher education in general. Business ethics is a traditional component of broader business-and-society courses and should continue to evolve with the field. However, those teaching business-ethics courses will usually find the coverage of this subject matter in a business-environment or business-and-society text insufficient to meet their needs.

The present abundance of business-ethics texts offers a much greater range of classroom material than was available a few years ago. This advantage, however, complicates the task of choosing among the available options. The choice can be especially confusing when an instructor has a weak background either in philosophy or in management practice.

There have been efforts to help sort through this confusion (Hanson 1983; Preston 1983; Pastin 1985). Hanson notes correctly that while texts written by professors of philosophy provide a solid philosophical foundation, this may be at the expense of the necessary management perspective on the complexity of management decision-making. Perhaps philosophy material is inherently difficult. Or perhaps the material in business ethics is simply different from usual business-school fare and for this very reason is necessary in the business curriculum. Pastin (1985) suggests that ethical questions may be intertwined with most of the topics and issues dealt with in business environment and that current interest in the area is a natural outgrowth of the subject matter treated in this part of the curriculum.

The heterogeneity of organizations has increased greatly with the inclusion of racial minorities and women and the blurring of social classes through mass education and affluence. The empowerment of groups previously disenfranchised in organizations has diminished the scope of shared values and ethics that previously could be assumed.

In addition, as each individual is bombarded by more and more information, he or she is exposed to varied and divergent value sets, ethical questions, and moral judgments. And, finally, the explosion of international economic issues in the past decades and the internationalization of the business curriculum provide a variety of new perspectives on values and behaviors.

Neither academics nor business practitioners should be surprised at the frequency of the call for more formal instruction in ethics. Values that used to be assumed are now open to question, not because of a deterioration in moral standards, but because of basic demographic changes in organizations and structural changes in society on both national and international levels. In a sense, it becomes the task of the management instructor to make plain to students that many work situations will call for ethical judgments, that good friends and honest coworkers may on occasion disagree about what constitutes a proper judgment, and that the consequences of inept ethical judgments may be just as disastrous for a corporation as inept judgments in finance or marketing.

CHAPTER 6

Pedagogical Approaches and Techniques

*Philip L. Cochran, John Mahon,
and Otis W. Baskin*

TEACHING APPROACHES AND TECHNIQUES

Teaching business environment is an intellectual challenge. Opinions differ regarding the appropriate subject matter and thematic focus. Business-and-society courses are sometimes expected to serve multiple purposes by program directors, deans, and other administrators. Some other major managerial disciplines have as their foundation a set of tools or procedures (e.g., internal rates of return or the Simplex Method) that are built upon in a careful sequence of courses. In business environment, as in policy and strategy, we have no such luxury. By its very nature, the course is integrative and comprehensive. As such, content, focus, and pedagogical techniques assume great significance. Three critical areas of concern are addressed here—the question of focus and content, the pedagogical approaches used, and written assignments and other ways to encourage student interest and creativity, which also serve as a basis for evaluation.

It should be noted at the outset, however, that good teaching, like many other skills, is perfected in practice. This being the case, those interested in improving their own teaching would be well advised to pursue these specific actions. First, sit in on the classes of other recognized good teachers, not to copy them, but to see how they handle classroom dynamics. This should include a discussion with the instructor prior to class as to what she/he expects to happen, what the goals and objectives are, and how this particular class fits in with the rest of the semester's coursework. After class, brief observations and the instructor's reactions to the assessment would complete the exercise.

Second, it can be illuminating to have others visit one's class, observe one's performance, and provide helpful criticism. Corollary to this, team teaching, while difficult administratively, can be helpful to a new (or seasoned) instructor in planning a curriculum and in actual classroom teaching.

Finally, opportunities to have class performance videotaped should not be missed. Watching oneself on television, while not always pleasant, is very revealing, both in terms of one's individual teaching mannerisms and of classroom dynamics.

Focus and Content

One possible range of choices regarding thematic content is shown in Table 6-1. For a fuller and somewhat different treatment see Wartick (1982). The choice of foci (internal or external, general or topical) is determined by the individual instructor. However, the variety of choices here suggests that, in a single required course in business environment, an instructor can either try to provide depth (concentrating on a single set of materials, e.g., external and general) or breadth (giving examples of all). The thrust of the course should also be a function of the level at which it is offered: undergraduate, MBA, or doctoral. At the doctoral level, attempts should be made to expose students to both the depth and breadth of the field. At the undergraduate and MBA levels, the breadth and depth of coverage may differ drastically, although MBA students should receive more in-depth coverage in selected areas. Buchholz (1979) has also addressed in detail the broad range of focus in these courses. Although focus varies, it is the instructor's responsibility to set the pace, direction, and content for her/his specific course.

Appendix 1 reproduces examples of syllabi used in this area, which reflect varying levels of depth and breadth of coverage. The courses represented are not intended to be definitive, but, as examples of approaches used at the MBA level, they demonstrate a variety of options.

Other appendices list textbooks in business environment and related texts (Appendix 2), texts in ethics (Appendix 3), and sources

Table 6–1. Alternative Curriculum Foci.

	External	Internal
General	*Systemic Context, Issues* Historical/Institutional Framework Major Social Trends Culture and Ideology	*Internal Context, Attitudes* Corporate Governance, Participation Management Ethics (Individual and Organizational)
	Ethics (broadly stated) *International Management*	
Topical	*Public Policy* Economic and Social Regulation Equal Employment Opportunity, Affirmative Action Environmental Protection	*Specific Management Policies/Techniques* Issue Management Environmental Scanning and Reporting Social Reporting

Source: Adapted from L.E. Preston, "Teaching Materials in Business and Society," *California Management Review* 25 (1983): 160.

of cases and videos (Appendixes 5 and 6). Again, these are by no means comprehensive lists, but they do suggest the range of available materials. Obviously, selection of materials is guided by the focus. It should be noted that subject matter seems to be shifting from topically oriented issues (consumerism, environmentalism) to more conceptual/theoretical offerings.

Pedagogical Issues

One of the most important decisions facing an instructor in this field concerns the method and materials to be used in the classroom. The choice should reflect instructional goals. Three distinct goals can be identified for analytical purposes: information acquisition, application of concepts to specific situations, and creativity, shown by new or unique approaches to problems and their definitions.

Providing information is the most basic aim of education. The preferred medium to achieve this goal is the lecture. This format is easy to master from an instructional standpoint, and student comprehension can be measured through the use of objective tests. One drawback to this teaching method is that it may not prepare the student well for application of the information to specific situations. The bright student will probably infer how to apply what she/he has learned, but little testing of applications will occur in the classroom/testing situation itself. This may be the best choice for an undergraduate program, where the primary goal will likely be to develop an awareness of issues and problems.

The next instructional goal is to give students opportunities to apply what they are learning to specific situations in business. The case method can be used here, perhaps supplemented with lectures. Comprehension and application skills can be measured in class through oral and written analyses of cases. This approach stimulates the practical application of theory, requiring students to define problems in managerially useful terms. The combination of information and application allows them to develop creative approaches to difficult problems and issues. On the negative side, it is difficult to assess student performance objectively, as can be done in the pure "information acquisition" approach. In addition, if careful thought is not given to case selection and the interweaving of lectures, students may find it difficult to grasp the focus and thrust of the course.

Unfortunately, the only background many students bring to courses in this area is their high-school civics course. This means that, regardless of the course focus, the instructor must provide frameworks and models to help students assimilate material. In addition, since few students will take jobs requiring the immediate use of these skills and techniques, the instructor must make especially clear the relevance of the material, not only to society, but to the practice of good management and the long-term survival of any organization.

It is generally accepted that application follows information acquisition. If this is so, this approach would seem to make most sense at the MBA level. One can assume that students at this level have been exposed to some of the issues and techniques in business and society, either through previous classwork at the undergraduate level or through business experience. The emphasis should rightly be, then, on the application of these materials to specific business and managerial situations. The challenge for the instructor is to provide a framework within which such analysis/application can occur, to develop a classroom atmosphere where risk taking is encouraged, and to demonstrate successfully that this knowledge/skill is an essential part of good, insightful management.

The final purpose of classroom instruction is to develop creativity so that students can come up with new ways to solve problems. This is obviously an extremely difficult task, and since the information and application stages should come first, a semester or quarter may not be sufficient to reach this level. Achievement of this level may also require a very high degree of curriculum integration. As a result, this level is most appropriate for doctoral studies, although it would also work well in small seminar situations and in those instances where an individual faculty member and a single student collaborate on a project.

Many of our colleagues assume that creativity is the goal of their instruction, but not all have thought through the full implications of such a goal nor recognized the preconditions of information acquisition and application experience. None of these goals for instruction is inferior; the instructor's choice will depend on the course objectives, the audience (i.e. undergraduate, graduate, doctoral), and the time allotted to business/society issues in the course itself and in the curriculum as a whole.

Table 6–2 summarizes some particulars of the three choices and adds two more: control and risk. In assessing instructive and testing techniques, the element of control and risk must also be considered. At the information stage, control of material, class, tone, etc., is clearly in the instructor's hands. Risk, however, lies with the student.

Table 6-2. Teaching Aims and Methods, Control, and Risk.

	Method of Instruction	Testing	Who Has Control?	Who Assumes Risk?
Information Acquisition	Lecture	Tests: Multiple Choice, true/false, fill-ins, etc.	Instructor	Student
Application	Case method/lecture	Oral written analysis of cases	Instructor/student	Instructor
Creativity	Small seminar/one on one	Term project, major paper, analysis	Instructor/student	Instructor/student

Source: John Mahon, Boston University, Boston, Massachusetts, 1986.

It is the student who can fail, answer incorrectly in class, and be embarrassed.

As teaching becomes more applications oriented, control is shared by both instructor and student. The instructor retains partial control, students can change the tone and direction of class by active participation and, in some cases, affect the selection of material in subsequent classes. Risk, however, shifts more to the instructor, as she/he loses rigid control of class direction and tone, and possibly the thematic focus as well. Here the instructor has to be flexible enough to go with the class in certain tangential directions, but firm enough to get back on track when necessary.

Finally, at the creativity level, collaborative efforts lead to a natural sharing of risk and control by both student and instructor. If creativity is to be encouraged, great flexibility and risk taking are required of all.

Assignments and Exercises

In-class activities, exercises, cases, outside projects, assignments, and examinations should support the considerations noted above. Interactive activities in the classroom to encourage debate and analysis of issues and problems from various viewpoints should be strongly encouraged. The use of student teams, who analyze given situations either through cases or projects and present their results to the class, is stimulating for both the students and the instructor.

Written assignments are, of course, of great value. The issue brief is a particularly useful exercise. A student or team of students examines a specific issue from the perspective of a given firm, going on to develop a comprehensive examination of the history of the issue, its current status, and any policy recommendations and/or contingency plans. (For a more complete description, see Wood's "Issues Briefs: Understanding the Business Environment," 1981.)

Alternatively, students can select for analysis an issue, a firm, an industry, or a proposed governmental action, agency, or regulatory body. The major requirements here are that, whatever is chosen, it must be current, and interviews of some of the main participants must be conducted. In this way, students are moved away from library research and forced to become more actively involved in their assignments. Students are expected to discuss the history, the major stakeholders, likely coalitions that may emerge, strategies of the actors involved, and a probable resolution.

Teaching business-and-society is stimulating. Part of the excitement comes from the continual need to apply one's analytical skills to ongoing issues in the business environment. Business, society, and government are constantly responding to and creating new problems and issues, which instructors in the field must take into consideration. Making sense of the plethora of topics and cases relevant to the business-and-society area is a constant challenge for instructors and students alike.

CHAPTER 7

Emergent Linkages of Business Environment with Business Ethics and Strategic Management

Karen Paul

The field of business environment, or business and public policy, or business and society, has existed as a recognizable subdiscipline of management for about twenty-five years (Preston 1986). During this time, study has tended to revolve around strongly topical issues and cases, which may have delayed the definition of a scholarly tradition, a shared paradigm, or even a set of common references to guide theory and research. However, within the past few years, certain themes have emerged around which the field seems to be coalescing. Two major streams of intellectual development can be identified—business ethics and strategic management—each of which offers a promising framework for creative theory building and solid research. In addition, there are several areas of management thought where application of a business-environment perspective seems uniquely appropriate and likely to contribute to managerial understanding. Among these is the study of international business, including the general societal and demographic contexts within which business does business, particularly the social problems associated with the creation of an enduring underclass. These problems are currently being given little attention within business environment, but may be increasingly important in future years.

BUSINESS ETHICS

The role of ethics and values is currently an important question in business and public policy. Two issues are involved. The first asks whether all problems should be framed as ethical questions, while the second relates to the usefulness of the ethical frame to develop particular recommendations for either corporate or public policy. A debate at the 1985 Academy of Management meetings exemplified the issues involved, and the protagonists later published their main points. Frederick supported the notion that the ethical dimension is central (Frederick 1986), while Vogel countered that many issues in business and public policy are simply pragmatic with very little if any inherent ethical content. At the meetings he cited the adoption of unit pricing by supermarkets, but his published statement presents rather more controversial examples (Vogel 1986).

On a certain crude level, the first position appears to be pro-ethics, while the latter seems to be pragmatic to the point of amorality. Yet Frederick's stance may be attacked as providing a means for critics of business to engage in mindless business bashing—or even thoughtful business bashing—under the guise of sound philosophical analysis. The second position is vulnerable to the charge that it serves to justify and rationalize any action in the best interest of business even at the cost of ethical judgment.

Vogel's championship of the latter position, however, contains a curious ambiguity, for he advocates almost in passing "increased intellectual exchange between students of corporate strategy and business ethics" (Vogel 1986: 143) and goes on to discuss the relationship of a firm's value system to its corporate culture and general level of performance. The chief argument against the use of ethics as an organizing motif would appear not to be an objection to ethics as such, but rather to the use of business ethics for the purpose of putting forth moralistic judgments based more on political convictions than on rigorous ethical analyses. Attributions of social responsibility often appear to coincide with the political biases of the person making the judgment. But it is hardly surprising that individuals have certain political preferences that at times may consciously or subconsciously influence their choice of problems, their analyses, and their policy recommendations. In fact, the effect of these factors on both scholarly analysis and public policy is well recognized (Horowitz 1972).

One further defense of the second position is that the limited diversity in the political preferences of those working in the field has fostered a homogeneity of opinion. The definition of problems and the identification of solutions tend to be consistent with the viewpoint of a 1970s-style liberal (Paul 1981–82; Vogel 1986). Many scholars have remained comfortably uninformed about the neoconservative philosophy and policy recommendations that have given form to the most significant public-policy changes of recent years. It is ironic that within the field of business environment the movement to limit the power and size of government, to support entrepreneurial activities, to encourage new forms of industry cooperation, and to espouse the efficiency of the market economy have been dealt with almost exclusively as political phenomena rather than as expressions of a philosophical movement transpiring not just in the United States but internationally and cross-culturally.

In suggesting this very point, Vogel undermines his own case by choosing less-than-convincing cases to illustrate possible applications of what he presents as the newer way of thinking, which, according to him, has now replaced 1970s-style liberalism as the guiding paradigm for public-policy analysis. He goes so far as to suggest that corporate aid for the Contras in Nicaragua and American corporate investment in South Africa could be considered ethically justifiable in light of the more contemporary moral framework. Vogel's premise deserves a more considered response than his examples are likely to inspire. A less inflammatory statement of the same basic issues has been made with the observation that, during the field's formative years, there had been a tremendous increase in laws and enforcement agencies intended to aim the business community toward socially desirable goals. Theoreticians and researchers in the field tended to project this trend out into the future with few qualifications, although there was some realization that not all of the public accepted the idea that government should control business more and more. On some level, it was recognized that social scientists, philosophers, and government officials had not yet developed the precise conceptualizations or methods of implementation that would produce the maximum social benefit on a predictable basis. Furthermore, a sizable part of the business community seemed downright reluctant to admit the legitimacy of these social demands, management statements about their social responsibility notwithstanding. However, despite these signs and the development of keen interest in neoconservative philosophy in many policymaking circles, business-environment scholars persisted in thinking that the inevitable wave of the future was more government control of business, more regulation, and more institutionalization of social goals within the business community. These assumptions needed to be reconsidered within the business environment field long before they were on any noticeable level (Paul 1981–82).

Frederick puts forth the position that all issues are ethical issues, that a frame of business ethics is fundamental to the business-environment field, essential for each and every analysis, and that other dimensions of analysis should necessarily come after the ethical dimension has been explored (1986). The normative orientation of the field was first expressed in terms of corporate social responsibility, then through the concept of corporate social responsiveness. Now, Frederick asserts, we are entering a new stage of thought on the social performance of corporations, a stage for which he has chosen the singularly unappealing label of "Corporate Social Rectitude (1986: 136). He says, "We want corporations to act with rectitude, to refer their policies and plans to a culture of ethics that embraces the most fundamental moral principles of humankind" (Frederick 1986: 136). But Frederick's use of the term "rectitude" carries a great deal of intellectual baggage. The corporation that employs social rectitude as a guiding principle must of necessity know what is righteous. Yet once one admits the possibility of different opinions as to right and wrong or the relative rightness of several alternative courses of action among which management must choose, rectitude as an organizing principle becomes unwieldy. Frederick does admit the difficulties of making these determinations in a pluralistic society, but avers that an effective corporate strategy regarding ethics can accommodate the differences natural in a complex and heterogeneous society. However, such a tone of arrogance or self-righteousness permeates his discussion that even his least controversial points end up generating resistance. Those who support even modest differences of opinion are accused of being unprincipled moral relativists whose ethical standards serve only the most pragmatic of interests.

The use of business ethics as *the* integrating concept for business environment or business and public policy seems to give the field an unnecessarily moralistic and prescriptive direction. However, the attempt to strip issues of ethical content is naive. Ethical content is inherent in all conscious human action of any significance. The incorporation of ethical considerations will not necessarily lead to any one set of analytic or policy outcomes. But to deny their relevance is to leave out those very considerations which may be of most significance for understanding the impact of both corporate and public policy.

STRATEGIC MANAGEMENT

Strategic management is another subject of much interest in business and public policy. Preston (1986), Vogel (1986), and others claim that a close linkage between these two fields provides the most intellectually satisfactory and the most pragmatically useful orientation for business and public policy. From this perspective, business and public policy becomes the component of the strategy-and-policy framework that focuses on changes in the political and economic environment, particularly on changing societal expectations. Ansoff (1979, 1984) and Freeman (1984) have produced texts on strategic management that have a strong external focus, while Tombari (1984) has published a business-and-society text strongly oriented toward strategic management.

Strategic management was developed as a subdiscipline before the business-environment tradition. Theorists and researchers in strategic management have been concerned predominantly with issues internal either to the firm or to the industry. The economic model of the corporation was generally accepted, with little effort devoted to identifying and planning for issues raised by consumer organizations, environmentalists, and other interest groups, which attracted so much attention in the formative years of the business-environment field. Applying a concept from systems theory, the strategic-management approach dismissed these elements as "noise," whereas they were either the central focus or an integral part of the analysis of company and industry problems in business environment.

Government policy was a consideration from the strategic management perspective, but, for quite a long time, the processes by which public policy is formulated and institutionalized and the ways in which companies can influence these processes have been relatively neglected within strategic management. Business environment, on the other hand, has attempted to identify important sources of political influence and to determine how public policy is developed—so much so that the label "Business and Public Policy" has now gained ascendancy over the more traditional "Business Environment."

Strategic management has relied heavily on the tools of conventional business analysis—those decisionmaking procedures within the firm that guide planning, implementation, and control of business functions—where business environment has used analytical and methodological approaches developed in a number of other fields, including law, political science, sociology, and philosophy. Strategic management has developed a strong disciplinary identification with several scholarly journals and rapidly growing academic associations. Business environment, however, is characterized by a somewhat less distinct disciplinary tradition; its journals tend to have multiple identities, publishing materials from a variety of fields, and membership in the field is growing slowly, if at all. Preston has suggested that this stage of development is characteristic of a discipline entering maturity (1986). If this is the case, perhaps business environment is prematurely aging. New intellectual lifeblood is vital to a field's continued growth and even to survival.

Although virtually every business school offers courses in business environment, centers of intellectual activity in the field are few and literally far between. Thus, business environment has trouble maintaining critical mass, a structural problem that does not exist for strategic management, where there are a number of universities where several or many scholars in the field are located.

The recent need to consider international competition as much as domestic, the difficulties faced by U.S.-based corporations in doing business on a global bases, and questions of national policy have necessarily compelled strategic management to adopt a more environmental focus. Numerous constraints on competition are governmentally imposed. Political pressure groups operating both inside and outside government assume increased importance in strategic analysis. In United Nations parlance, NGOs (non-governmental organizations) and PVOs (private voluntary organizations) exercise a somewhat unpredictable and potentially quite troublesome (to the corporation) influence on political processes, in the media, and in the formation of public opinion, on both a national and international level (Sethi 1986). All of these developments make necessary a more environmental perspective.

However, the difficulties corporations now face from the intensity of global competition make it questionable whether the strategic-management framework can maintain even a modicum of regard for questions of justice and fairness. The ideal of social responsibility has been accepted in strategic management mainly on pragmatic grounds, on the basis that it pays in the long run. But that assumption is increasingly less inevitable, especially on the international level. As the attempt to become more and more competitive becomes the dominant driving force, consideration of the citizenship role of the corporation may decline, at the expense of strategic management's contribution to business environment, and vice versa. Interest in how responsible management of the corporation can maximize benefits in a holistic way could give way to strictly economic questions of competition. At that point, interconnection of the two fields would be limited to those areas concerned with issues management, the structure of public-affairs offices, advocacy advertising, and other ways in which the corporation can mold public opinion and political processes.

On the other hand, from a more macro point of view, problems of intense competition arise mainly from the undercapacity of the world's societies to absorb the production of corporations and other economic institutions, such as small business and agricultural enterprise. Solving these problems will require, as indeed it always has, that root causes—in this case, gross global inequities in the distribution of goods, the institutionalization of poverty, and the creation of an underclass even in prosperous societies, and more—be set right. Corporations cannot do this alone, but they can play a leading role in pushing society towards confrontation of structural issues that make it difficult to do business. Even the most astute management of any corporation cannot compensate for gross societal deficiencies, just as it cannot fail to deal with the political realities that are created by these conditions.

These latter points lead to the recognition that the most traditional of business-environment topics, those having to do with poverty and discrimination, may be in for a resurgence of interest in coming years. In order for the corporation to compete effectively on a world scale, mere manipulation of public opinion and political processes will not suffice to ensure effective performance. Rather, some degree of concern with the fairness and justice of the institutional fabric of societies will be essential, if only for purely pragmatic reasons. It is in this area that the fields of business environment and strategic management have the greatest potential for meaningful linkage.

A PARADOX

An interesting paradox emerges when one considers the linkages of business environment with both business ethics and strategic management. As long as an issue is emerging, not yet clearly attached to one of the functional areas of business, it is an ideal candidate for study within the business-environment framework. Then the normal course of events may bring the issue to the attention of the federal government, or the courts, or industry associations, or professional groups, and policies emerge, quite likely institutionalized in some legal form or else as an industry code.

Within corporations, areas are beginning to be defined where such emergent issues are analyzed, as in the newly developing field of issues management. But what issues are to be addressed, what types of analysis are appropriate, and by what yardstick are results to be measured? Difficult questions, and yet revealing. The title *The Unstable Ground* (Sethi 1974) was coined to reflect the alleged changeability of the environmental ground on which the contemporary corporation stands. But perhaps that phrase describes just as aptly the field of business environment, with its subject matter that by nature shifts from topical issue to topical issue and its problems that move to other areas of management—perhaps personnel, or business law, or accounting, or finance—or into the framework of political science, economics, or international studies as soon as they are resolved (as much as management problems are ever resolved). Perhaps business environment serves as an early warning device in management thought and to corporations. It may be regrettable that an enduring body of theory and a generally accepted tradition of empirical research is so difficult to define for business environment. Contributions from and to the fields of business ethics and strategic management may help to remedy this gap. At the same time, the main strength of business environment has been the relevance and significance of its subject matter, which continues to characterize the field.

Appendixes

Sample Course Outlines

1. Business and Society: Current Issues
2. Business and Society: Issues and Ideologies
3. The Interaction of Business and Government
4. Context of the Business System
5. Managing Business-Government Relations
6. Business and Public Policy: Political Strategies
7. Management Policy II
8. Business and Public Policy: Theory and Practice
9. Management and Ethics
10. Business Ethics

1. BUSINESS AND SOCIETY: CURRENT ISSUES

I. The business and society relationship

   A. An overview of the business-society relationship
   B. From social responsibility to social responsiveness
   C. Business ethics and management

II. External publics and issues

   A. Business and government
   B. Business and the consumer
   C. Business and the environment
   D. Business and the community

III. Internal publics and issues

   A. Business, employees, and the individual
   B. Business and employment discrimination
   C. Business, ownership, and corporate governance

IV. Managing corporate social performance

   A. Corporate social policy and management
   B. Planning and organizing for social response
   C. Social performance measurement and auditing
   D. Communicating the business social role

V. The future social role of business

We are indebted to Professor Archie B. Carroll, University of Georgia, for suggestions on this approach.

2.   BUSINESS AND SOCIETY: ISSUES AND IDEOLOGIES

Introduction

I.   American business history
II.   Environmentalism
III.   Consumerism
IV.   Employee issues
V.   Corporate governance
VI.   Media relations
VII.   Business-government relations
VIII. Antitrust
IX.   Marxist ideology
X.   Neoconservative ideology
XI.   Public policy development
XII.   Business ethics
XIII. International dimensions
XIV.   Issues management
XV.   Technological assessment

We are indebted to Professor Philip Cochran, Pennsylvania State University, for suggestions on this approach.

3. THE INTERACTION OF BUSINESS AND GOVERNMENT

I. Political economy and the role of the state

   A. Basic issues
   B. The nature of political economy
   C. United States models of business-government interaction

II. An historical perspective of government-business relations

   A. A functional typology (see IIIB)
   B. Pre-Civil War period
   C. Post-Civil War period

III. The contemporary era

   A. Advanced industrial capitalist political economy in the United States
   B. Interactions between government and business
      1. Sponsorship and risk taking
      2. Planning and economic management
      3. Allocation of tangible and intangible property interests
      4. Purchasing
      5. Stabilization
      6. Regulation and deregulation
      7. Collaboration and joint ventures
      8. Taxation

IV. Business and politics

   A. Governmental policies
   B. Electoral politics

V. Future directions of government-business interaction

   A. Other advanced industrial nations
   B. Alternatives and possibilities in the United States

We are indebted to Professor Edwin Epstein, University of California at Berkeley, for suggestions on this approach.

4. CONTEXT OF THE BUSINESS SYSTEM

I. Capitalism—mercantile and managerial

   A. History and evolution of capitalism
   B. The managerial revolution

II. Capitalism—ideology and survival

   A. The political and social concomitants of capitalism
   B. Market theories

III. Business and government—political processes

   A. Electoral influence
   B. "Hidden" influence

IV. Regulation

V. Corporations—governance and responsibilities

VI. Workers and unions

VII. Justice and ethics

VIII. International issues

We are indebted to Professor Dennis Quinn and Professor Thomas M. Jones, University of Washington, for suggestions on this approach.

5. MANAGING BUSINESS-GOVERNMENT RELATIONS

I. Introduction

    A. Typical problems
    B. Consolidated Edison case

II. The government decisionmaking process

    A. Key participants
    B. Developmental cycle
    C. Costs and benefits
    D. Selected cases

III. Managing business-government relationships

    A. Allied Chemical case
    B. EPA case
    C. Procter & Gamble—FTC case
    D. Equal employment opportunity—AT&T case
    E. Gulf Oil case

IV. Managing joint business-governmental projects

V. Managing relationships among business, interest groups, and the public

    A. Illinois Power case
    B. Chain saws case
    C. National Coal Policy project

We are indebted to Professor J. Ronald Fox, Harvard Business School, for suggestions on this approach.

6. BUSINESS AND PUBLIC POLICY: POLITICAL STRATEGIES

I. Social issues and public policy

   A. Conceptual perspectives
   B. Trade-offs and trends in economic policies
   C. Trade-offs and trends in law and policies

II. The political process

   A. Congress—structure, decisionmaking, and public policy
   B. Regulation—politics and decisionmaking
   C. Elections—campaigns and strategy
   D. Elections—voters, politics, and participation

III. Participation in the political process

   A. Interest groups and politics
   B. Money, politics, and public policy
   C. Corporate political participation
   D. The legitimacy of corporate political action

IV. Selected cases

We are indebted to Professor Gerald Keim, Texas A&M, for suggestions on this approach.

7. MANAGEMENT POLICY II

I. Introduction: The business-government-society relationship

   A. Environmental scanning and analysis
   B. Corporate strategies
   C. Selected cases

II. The public impact of business—critical issues

   A. Private decisions and public consequences
   B. Managerial choices
      1. Private sector
      2. Public sector
   C. Issue life cycles and managerial discretion
   D. Internal implementation of social policies
   E. Selected cases

III. The public-policy process

   A. The role of legislation/legislature
   B. Regulating agencies and discretionary power
   C. The role of the media

IV. Conflict and collaboration

   A. The internal corporate agenda
   B. Industrial policies
   C. Foreign government policy
   D. Form of investment/negotiating entry
   E. Selected cases

V. Business-governmental-society relationships in transition

   A. Project management and stakeholder analysis
   B. Evolving political strategies and issues

Please note: This course follows Management Policy I, which focuses on market and industry elements or forces operating on a firm.

We are indebted to Professor John Mahon, Boston University, for suggestions on this approach.

8. BUSINESS AND PUBLIC POLICY: THEORY AND PRACTICE

I. Introduction

II. Concepts, theories, and models

A. Private management and public policy
B. The corporate form evolves
C. Corporate performance and public trust
D. Corporate governance
E. Selected cases

III. Policy process

A. Theory
B. Examples: energy; industrial policy
C. Selected cases

IV. Government regulation

A. Antitrust regulation
B. Economic regulation
C. Social regulation
D. Selected cases

V. Business-government relations

A. Public affairs management
B. Community relations/philanthropy
C. Political issues and processes
D. Selected cases

VI. The multinational

VIII. Trends for the future

We are indebted to Professor Lee Preston, University of Maryland, for suggestions on this approach.

9. MANAGEMENT AND ETHICS

I. Ethics and business
II. Ethical reasoning
III. Individual and corporation
IV. Individual and corporate culture
V. Employee rights and welfare
VI. The individual as change agent
VII. Middle managers
VIII. Corporate moral responsibility
IX. Policy issues
X. Controlling employee behavior
XI. Incentives for ethical behavior
XII. Implementing corporate ethics
XIII. Leadership
XIV. Religious critique of capitalism
XV. Marxist critique of capitalism
XVI. University ethics

We are indebted to Professor Kirk Hanson, Stanford University, for suggestions on this approach.

10. BUSINESS ETHICS

I. Ethical theory

    A. Relativism
    B. Utilitarianism
    C. Moral development
    D. Deontology and rights
    E. Libertarianism
    F. Justice as fairness

II. Historical roots

    A. Biblical
    B. Medieval
    C. Luther
    D. Christian vocation
    E. Calvin
    F. Weber
    G. English Puritanism
    H. Carnegie
    I. Laissez-faire
    J. Social Gospel

III. Economic theory

    A. Adam Smith
    B. Marx and Engels
    C. Malthus and Ricardo
    D. Spenser and Sumner

IV. Ethics application

    A. Ethics in the workplace
    B. Ethics in the marketplace
    C. Multinationals and morality
    D. The new moral imperative for business

We are indebted to Professor Walter Benjamin, Hamline University, for this approach.

APPENDIX 2

Teaching Materials: Business Environment, Business and Society, and Social Issues

Major Texts

Aram, J. D. *Managing Business and Public Policy: Concepts, Issues, and Cases.* 2nd ed. Marshfield, Mass.: Pitman Publishing, 1986.

Buchholz, R. A. *Business Environment and Public Policy: Implications for Management.* Englewood Cliffs, N.J.: Prentice-Hall, 1982.

Carroll, A. B. *Business and Society: Managing Corporate Social Performance.* Boston: Little, Brown, 1981.

Davis, K., and W. C. Frederick. *Business and Society: Management, Public Policy, Ethics.* 5th ed. New York: McGraw-Hill, 1984.

Fox, J. R. *Managing Business-Government Relations: Cases and Notes on Business-Government Problems.* Homewood, Ill.: Richard D. Irwin, 1982.

Greer, D. F. *Business, Government and Society.* New York: Macmillan, 1983.

Hysom, J. L. and W. J. Bolce. *Business and Its Environment.* St. Paul, Minn.: West Publishing, 1983.

Luthans, F., R. M. Hodgetts, and K. R. Thompson. *Social Issues in Business: Strategic and Public Policy Perspectives.* 4th ed. New York: Macmillan, 1984.

McFarland, D. E. *Management and Society: An Institutional Framework.* Englewood Cliffs, N.J.: Prentice-Hall, 1982.

Sawyer, G. C. *Business and Society: Managing Corporate Social Impact.* 2nd ed. Englewood Cliffs, N.J.: Prentice-Hall, 1985.

Starling, G. *The Changing Environment of Business: A Managerial Approach.* 2nd ed. Boston: Kent Publishing, 1980.

Steiner, G. A., and J. D. Steiner. *Business, Government & Society: A Managerial Perspective.* 4th ed. New York: Random House, 1985.

_____. *Issues in Business and Society.* 2nd ed. New York: Random House, 1980.

Sturdivant, F. D. *Business and Society: A Managerial Approach.* 3rd ed. Homewood, Ill.: Richard D. Irwin, 1985.

Sturdivant, F. D., and L. M. Robinson. *The Corporate Social Challenge: Cases and Commentaries.* Revised ed. Homewood, Ill.: Richard D. Irwin, 1981.

Tombari, H. A. *Business & Society.* Hinsdale, Ill.: Dryden Press, 1984.

Please note that many of these texts were reviewed by Lee Preston in his book review in the *California Management Review* (vol. 25, no. 3, spring 1983).

Related Texts

Aguilar, F. J. *Scanning The Business Environment.* New York: Macmillan, 1967.

Aldrich, H. *Organizations and Environments.* Englewood Cliffs, N.J.: Prentice-Hall, 1979.

Ahorini, Y. *Financing Politics.* Chatham, N.J.: Chatham Press, 1981.

Alexander, H. *Financing Politics.* Washington, D.C.: Congressional Quarterly Press, 1984.

Bradshaw, T., and D. Vogel, eds. *Corporations and Their Critics.* New York: McGraw-Hill, 1980.

Braybrooke, D., and C. Lindblom. *A Strategy of Decision.* New York: Free Press, 1970.

Buchholz, R. A. *The Essentials of Public Policy for Management.* Englewood Cliffs, N.J.: Prentice-Hall, 1985.

Buchholz, R. A., W. D. Evans, and R. A. Wagley. *Management Response to Public Issues: Concepts & Cases in Strategy Formulation.* Englewood Cliffs, N.J.: Prentice-Hall, 1985.

Carroll, A. B. *Managing Corporate Social Responsibility.* Boston: Little, Brown, 1977.

Cohn, J. *The Conscience of the Corporations: Business and Urban Affairs 1967–1970.* Baltimore, Md. Johns Hopkins University Press, 1971.

Cigler, A. and B. A. Loomis, eds. *Interest Group Politics.* Washington, D.C.: Congressional Quarterly Press, 1983.

Dunlop, J. T., ed. *Business and Public Policy.* Cambridge: Harvard University Press, 1981.

Edelman, M. *The Symbolic Uses of Politics.* Chicago: University of Illinois Press, 1964.

Elkins, A. and D. W. Callaghan. *A Managerial Odyssey: Problems in Business and its Environment.* 3rd ed. Reading, Mass.: Addison-Wesley, 1981.

Epstein, E. *The Corporation in American Politics.* Englewood Cliffs, N.J.: Prentice-Hall, 1969.

Eyestone, R. *From Social Issues to Public Policy.* New York: John Wiley & Sons, 1978.

Ewing, D. W. *Freedom Inside the Organization.* New York: McGraw-Hill, 1977.

Freeman, R. E. *Strategic Management*, Marshfield, Mass.: Pitman Publishing, 1984.

Galambos, L. *The Public Image of Big Business in America 1880–1940.* London: Johns Hopkins University Press, 1975.

Gibans, N. F. *The Community Arts Council Movement.* New York: Praeger Publishers, 1982.

Gollner, A. B. *Social Change and Corporate Strategy.* Stamford, Conn.: Issue Action Publications, 1983.

Grefe, E. A. *Fighting to Win: Business Political Power.* New York: Harcourt Brace Jovanovich, 1981.

Heald, M. *The Social Responsibility of Business: Company and Community 1900–1960.* Cleveland, Ohio: Case Western Reserve University Press, 1970.

Huenefeld, J. *The Community Activist's Handbook.* Boston: Beacon Press, 1970.

Jacobsen, G. *The Politics of Congressional Elections.* Boston: Little, Brown, 1983.

Koch, F. *The New Corporate Philanthropy.* New York: Plenum Press, 1979.

Lindblom, C. E. *Politics and Markets.* New York: Basic Books, 1977.

MacMillan, I. *Strategy Formulation: Political Concepts.* St. Paul, Minn.: West Publishing, 1978.

Mitnik, B. M. *The Political Economy of Regulation.* New York: Columbia University Press, 1980.

Molander, E. A. *Responsive Capitalism: Case Studies in Corporate Social Conduct.* New York: McGraw-Hill, 1980.

Nagelschmidt, J. S., ed. *The Public Affairs Handbook.* New York: AMACOM, 1982.

Oleszek, W. J. *Congressional Procedures and the Policy Process.* Washington, D.C.: Congressional Quarterly Press, 1984.

Olson, M. *The Logic of Collective Action: Public Goods and the Theory of Groups.* Cambridge: Harvard University Press, 1965.

Pastin, M. *The Hard Problems of Management: Gaining the Ethics Edge.* San Francisco: Jossey-Bass, 1986.

Pfeffer, J., and G. Salancik. *The External Control of Organizations.* New York: Harper & Row, 1978.

Post, J. E. *Corporate Behavior and Social Change.* Reston, Va.: Reston Publishing, 1978.

Post, J. E., and J. F. *Corporate Public Affairs.* Marshfield, Mass.: Pitman Publishing, 1985.

Preston, L. E., ed. *Research in Corporate Social Performance and Policy.* Vols. 1–9. Greenwich, Conn.: JAI Press, 1978, 1980, 1981, 1982, 1983, 1984, 1985, 1986, and 1987.

Preston, L. E., and J. E. Post. *Private Management and Public Policy.* Englewood Cliffs, N.J.: Prentice-Hall, 1975.

Raines, J. C., L. E. Berson, and D. McI. Gracie. *Community and Capital in Conflict: Plant Closings and Job Loss.* Philadelphia: Temple University Press, 1982.

Rosenbaum, W. A. *Energy, Politics and Public Policy.* Washington, D.C.: Congressional Quarterly, 1981.

Schattschneider, E. E. *The Semi-Sovereign People.* New York: Hold, Rinehart, & Winston, 1960.

Schultze, C. L. *The Public Use of Private Interest.* Washington, D.C.: The Brookings Institution, 1977.

Sethi, S. P. *Up Against The Corporate Wall: Modern Corporations and Social Issues of the Eighties.* 4th ed. Englewood Cliffs, N.J.: Prentice-Hall, 1982.

Sethi, S. P., and C. L. Swanson. *Private Enterprise and Public Purpose: An Understanding of the Role of Business in a Changing Social System.* New York: John Wiley & Sons, 1981.

Shipper, F., and M. M. Jennings. *Business Strategy for the Political Arena.* Westport, Conn.: Greenwood Press, 1984.

Sonnenfield, J. A. *Corporate Views of the Public Interest: Perceptions of the Forest Products Industry.* Boston: Auburn House, 1981.

Sowell, T. *Knowledge and Decisions.* New York: Basic Books, 1980.

Starling, G., and O. Baskin. *Issues in Business and Society: Capitalism and the Public Purpose.* Boston, Mass.: Kent Publishing, 1985.

Steckmest, F. W. *Corporate Performance.* New York: McGraw-Hill, 1982.

Stone, C. D. *Where The Law Ends: The Social Control of Corporate Behavior.* New York: Harper & Row, 1975.

Toffler, B. L. *Tough Choices: Managers Talk Ethics.* New York: John Wiley, 1986.

Vogel, D. *Lobbying the Corporation.* New York: Basic Books, 1978.

Weidenbaum, M. L. *Business Government and The Public.* 2nd ed. Englewood Cliffs, N.J.: Prentice-Hall, 1981.

Westin, A. F., ed. *Whistleblowing: Loyalty and Dissent in the Corporation.* New York: McGraw-Hill, 1981.

APPENDIX 3

Business Ethics Materials

Texts Without Cases

Benson, G. C. S. *Business Ethics in America.* Lexington, Mass.: D.C. Heath, 1982.

Bowie, N. *Business Ethics.* Englewood Cliffs, N.J.: Prentice-Hall, 1982.

Braybrooke, D. *Ethics in the World of Business.* Totowa, N.J.: Rowman & Littlefield, 1983.

DeGeorge, R. T. *Business Ethics.* New York: Macmillan, 1982.

DeGeorge, R. T., and J. A. Pichler, eds. *Ethics, Free Enterprise, and Public Policy: Original Essays on Moral Issues in Business.* New York: Oxford University Press, 1978.

Donaldson, T. *Corporations & Morality.* Englewood Cliffs, N.J.: Prentice-Hall, 1982.

Evans, W. S. *Management Ethics: An Intercultural Perspective.* Norwell, Mass.: Kluwer-Nijhoff, 1981.

Garrett, T. M. *Business Ethics.* New York: Appleton-Century-Crofts, 1966.

Missner, M. *Ethics of the Business System.* Sherman Oaks, Calif. Alfred Publishing, 1980.

Texts With Cases

Barry, V. *Moral Issues in Business.* 2nd ed. Belmont, Calif.: Wadsworth Publishing, 1983.

Beauchamp, T. L., and N. E. Bowie. *Ethical Theory and Business.* 2nd ed. Englewood Cliffs, N.J.: Prentice-Hall, 1983.

DesJardins, J. R., and J. J. McCall. *Contemporary Issues in Business Ethics.* Belmont, Calif.: Wadsworth Publishing, 1985.

Donaldson, T., and P. H. Werhane. *Ethical Issues in Business.* 2nd ed. Englewood Cliffs, N. J.: Prentice-Hall, 1983.

Hoffman, W. M., and J. M. Moore. *Business Ethics.* New York: McGraw-Hill, 1984.

McCoy, C. S. *Management of Values: The Ethical Difference in Corporate Policy and Performance.* Boston: Pitman Publishing, 1985.

Smith, G. A., Jr., and J. B. Matthews, Jr. *Business, Society, and the Individual.* Homewood, Ill.: Richard D. Irwin, 1967.

Soleman, R. C., and K. R. Hanson. *Above the Bottom Line: An Introduction to Business Ethics.* New York: Harcourt Brace Jovanovich, 1983.

Snoeyenbos, M., R. Almeder, and J. Humber. *Business Ethics: Corporate Values and Society.* Buffalo, N.Y.: Prometheus Books, 1983.

Velasquez, M. G. *Business Ethics: Concepts and Cases.* Englewood Cliffs, N.J.: Prentice-Hall, 1982.

Case Books

Beauchamp, T. L. *Case Studies in Business, Society and Ethics.* Englewood Cliffs, N.J.: Prentice-Hall, 1983.

Donaldson, T. *Case Studies in Business Ethics.* Englewood Cliffs, N.J.: Prentice-Hall, 1984.

Glenn, J. R., Jr. *Ethics in Decision Making.* New York: John Wiley & Sons, 1986.

Hay, R. D., and E. R. Gray. *Business and Society: Cases and Text.* 2nd ed. Cincinnati: Southwestern Publishing, 1981.

Matthews, J. B., K. E. Goodpastor, and L. N. Nash. *Policies and Persons: A Casebook in Business Ethics.* New York: McGraw-Hill, 1985.

Supplementary Books

Baumhart, R. C. *An Honest Profit.* New York: Holt, Rinehart, & Winston, 1968.

Blackburn, T. *Christian Business Ethics: Doing Good While Doing Well.* Chicago: Fides/Claretian, 1981.

Cavanagh, G. F. *American Business Values in Transition.* 1st and 2nd eds. Englewood Cliffs, N.J.: Prentice-Hall, 1976, 1984.

Elbing, A. O., Jr., and C. J. Elbing. *The Value Issue of Business.* New York: McGraw-Hill, 1967.

Hoffman, W. M., J. M. Moore, and D. A. Fedo, eds. *Corporate Governance and Institutional Ethics.* Proceedings of the Fifth National Conference on Business Ethics. Lexington, Mass.: D.C. Heath, 1984.

Jones, D.G., ed. *Doing Ethics in Business.* Cambridge, Mass.: Oelgeschlager, Gunn, Hain, 1982.

Southard, S. *Ethics for Executives.* Nashville, Tenn.: Thomas Nelson, 1975.

Williams, O. F., and J. W. Houck. *Full Value: Cases in Christian Business Ethics.* New York: Harper & Row, 1978.

______. *The Judeo-Christian Vision and the Modern Corporation.* Notre Dame, Ind.: University of Notre Dame Press, 1982.

Business Ethics Organizations

Center for Business, Society and Ethics
Carlow College
3333 Fifth Avenue
Pittsburgh, PA 15213
(412) 578-6053
Peter Madsen, director

Center for Business Ethics
Bentley College
Waltham, MA
(617) 891-2115
Michael Hoffman, director

Center for Corporate Concern
218 Wagley Hall
Wright State University
Dayton, OH 45435
(513) 873-3304
Alan B. Cooper, director

Center for Public and Private Ethics
Arizona State University
Tempe, AZ 85187
(602) 965-2895
Mark Pastin, director

Center for the Study of Applied Ethics
Box 6550
Darden Graduate School of Business
University of Virginia
Charlottesville, VA 22906
(804) 924-7248
Alexander B. Horniman, director

Center for the Study of Ethics
 in the Professions
Illinois Institute of Technology
Chicago, IL 60616
(312) 567-3017
Mark Frankel, director

Center for the Study of Values
University of Delaware
Newark, DE 19711
(302) 738-2546
Norman E. Bowie, director

Ethics Resource Center
1730 Rhode Island Ave.
Washington, DC 20036
(202) 223-3411
Gary Edwards, director

Hastings Center
360 Broadway
Hastings-on-Hudson, NY 10706
(914) 475-0500
Daniel Callahan, director

Society for Business Ethics
820 N. Michigan Ave.
Chicago, IL 60611
(312) 274-3000
Patricia Werhane, director

APPENDIX 5

Case Material Sources

There are four major sources of case material, some of which are not very well known.

1. The biggest and best known, HBS Case Services, Harvard Business School, Boston, MA 02163 publish extensive bibliographies of case material and package cases and materials around certain themes (e.g., an "Ethics in Management" package of Goodpaster).

2. Lesser known, but possessing a very interesting array of cases that apply to this field, is the Public Policy and Management Programs, housed in the School of Management at Boston University, 621 Commonwealth Ave., Boston, MA 02215. Sections in their bibliography deal with political and institutional analysis and ethical and moral issues.

3. Robert Ronstadt, of Babson College in Wellesley, Massachusetts, has developed another case distribution service called Case Teachers Association (CAT), which offers cases in a variety of areas. The publisher is Lord Publishing, 46 Glen Street, Dover, MA 02030, from whom a case collection catalogue can be obtained.

4. *The Journal of Management Case Studies* is a new publication from Elsevier Science Publishing, 52 Vanderbilt Avenue, New York, NY 10017.

Other Materials

1. Another source of materials germane to this area is the Issues Management Association at 1090 Vermont Ave., N.W., Rm. 928, Washington, DC 20005.

2. A thorough survey of teaching materials (although becoming dated) can be found in Buchholz's *Business Environment and Public Policy: A Study of Teaching and Research.* Available from AACSB, 605 Old Ballas Road, St. Louis, MO 63141.

3. A teaching module dealing with public relations/public affairs management is being prepared for distribution by the Foundation for Public Relations Research and Education. The module, consisting of readings, simulations, exercises, and case studies, has been prepared by Otis Baskin and Grover Starling specifically for graduate business programs. Distribution information is available from the Foundation for Public Relations Research and Education, Suite 1816, 310 Madison Ave., New York, NY 10017.

4. Many excellent video materials, most useful in teaching, are available. However, these typically become outdated quickly, so we have refrained from making specific recommendations. Rather, we suggest referring to current newsletters and reviews as an ongoing source of information on topical material. For example, the newsletter for the Social Issues in Management Division of the Academy of Management often carries reviews of video material.

Bibliography

Ackerman, R. W. "How Companies Respond to Social Demands." *Harvard Business Review* 51 (1973): 88–98.

______. *The Social Challenge to Business.* Cambridge: Harvard University Press, 1975.

Ackerman, R. W., and A. Bauer. *Corporate Social Responsiveness.* Reston, Va.: Reston Publishing, 1976.

Ajuogu, M. O. "Ethical Dilemma of Public Sector Executives in a Developing Economy." Paper presented at the 42d Annual Meeting of the Academy of Management, New York, 1982.

American Assembly of Collegiate Schools of Business. *Faculty Requirements and Standards in Collegiate Schools of Business.* New York: American Assembly of Collegiate Schools of Business, 1955.

______. *Accreditation Council Policies, Procedures, and Standards 1986–87.* St. Louis, Mo.: American Assembly of Collegiate Schools of Business, 1986.

Andrews, K. R. "Can the Best Corporations Be Made Moral?" *Harvard Business Review* 51 (1973): 57–64.

Anshen, M. *Managing the Socially Responsible Corporation.* New York: Macmillan, 1974.

Ansoff, H. I. *Strategic Management.* New York: John Wiley & Sons, 1979.

______. *Implanting Strategic Management.* Englewood Cliffs, N.J.: Prentice-Hall, 1984.

Aram, J. D. *Managing Business and Public Policy.* 2d ed. Marshfield, Mass.: Pitman, 1983.

Arlow, P., and T. A. Ulrich. "Are Proposals to Improve Business Ethics Effective? An Assessment by Business Graduates and Executives." Paper presented at the 44th Annual Meeting of the Academy of Management, Boston, 1984.

______ . "Business Ethics and Business School Graduates: A Longitudinal Study." *Akron Business and Economic Review* 16 (1985): 13–17.

Arrow, K. J. *Social Choice and Individual Values.* New Haven, Conn.: Yale University Press, 1951.

Arthur Andersen. *Cost of Government Regulation.* New York: The Business Roundtable, 1979.

Barach, J. A., and E. A. Nicol. "Teaching Ethics in Business School." *Collegiate News and Views* 34 (Fall 1980): 5–8.

Barnard, C. I. *The Functions of the Executive.* Cambridge: Harvard University Press, 1938.

Barry, V. *Moral Issues in Business.* Belmont, Calif.: Wadsworth Publishing, 1979.

Bauer, R. A., and D. H. Fenn, Jr. *The Corporate Social Audit.* New York: Russel Sage Foundation, 1972.

Baumhart, R. *An Honest Profit.* New York: Holt, Rinehart & Winston, 1968.

______ . "How Ethical Are Businessmen?" *Harvard Business Review* (July 1961): 6–19 (August 1961): 156–66.

Beauchamp, T. L., and N. E. Bowie. *Ethical Theory and Business.* 2d ed. Englewood Cliffs, N. J.: Prentice-Hall, 1983.

Bond, K. M. *Bibliography of Business Ethics and Business Moral Values.* Omaha, Nebr.: Creighton University, 1984.

Boulding, K. E. "Religious Foundations of Economic Progress." *Harvard Business Reviews* 30 (1952): 33–40.

______ . *The Organizational Revolution.* New York: Harper & Brothers, 1953.

Bowen, R. H. *Social Responsibility of the Businessman.* New York: Harper & Brothers, 1953.

Bowie, N. *Business Ethics.* Englewood Cliffs, N. J.: Prentice-Hall, 1982.

Boyer, E. *College: The Undergraduate Experience in America.* New York: Harper & Row, 1987.

Bremer, O. A. "Is Business the Source of Social Values?" *Harvard Business Review* 49 (1971): 121–26.

______ . "Ethical Decisions in Capitalist Structures." *The Forum, Association for Social Economics Journal* (1978): 34–35.

______ . "Religious Insights in Management Decision Making." Paper presented at the Western Academy of Management, Monterey, Calif., 1981.

Broehl, W. G., Jr. "Looking Around: Do Business and Religion Mix? *Harvard Business Review* 36 (1958): 139–44.

Buchholz, R. A. *Business Environment/Public Policy: A Study of Teaching and Research in Schools of Business and Management.* St. Louis, Mo.: Washington University Center for the Study of American Business, 1979.

Bunting, J. W., ed. *Ethics for Modern Business Practice.* Englewood Cliffs, N.J.: Prentice-Hall, 1953.

Campbell, T. C., Jr. "Capitalism and Christianity." *Harvard Business Review* 35 (1957): 37–44.

Cavanagh, G. F. *American Business Values in Transition.* 2d ed. Englewood Cliffs, N.J.: Prentice-Hall, 1984.

Center for Business Ethics. *A Selected Bibliography of Business Ethics Books.* Waltham, Mass.: Bentley College, 1978.

Chamberlain, N. W. *The Limits of Corporate Responsibility.* New York: Basic Books, 1973.

Chatov, R. "The Role of Ideology in the American Corporation." In D. Votow and S. P. Sethi, eds., *The Corporate Dilemma*, pp. 50–73. Englewood Cliffs, N.J.: Prentice-Hall, 1973.

Cheit, E. F. "Why Managers Cultivate Social Responsibility." *California Management Review* 7 (1964): 3–22.

____. "What Is the Field of Business and Society and Where Is It Going?" *AACSB Bulletin* 11 (1975): 17–19.

Childs, M. W., and D. Cater. *Ethics in a Business Society.* New York: Harper & Brothers, 1954.

Clark, W. C. *Religion and the Moral Standards of American Businessmen.* Cincinnati: Southwestern Publishing, 1966.

Committee for Education in Business Ethics. *Report of the Committee for Education in Business Ethics.* Skokie, Ill.: 1980.

Conrad, M. R. "Are Business Ethics Worth Studying?" *Business and Society Review* no. 27 (1978): 54–57.

Corson, J. J., and G. A. Steiner. *Measuring Business's Social Performance: The Corporate Social Audit.* New York: Committee for Economic Development, 1974.

David, D. K. "Business Responsibilities in an Uncertain World." *Harvard Business Review* 27 (1949): 1–8.

Davis, K. "Can Business Afford to Ignore Social Responsibilities?" *California Management Review* 2 (1960): 70–76.

____. "The Public Role of Management." Presidential address at the Annual Meeting of the Academy of Management, Boston, 1965.

Davis, K., and Blomstrom, R. E. *Business and Its Environment.* 2d ed. New York: McGraw-Hill, 1976.

Davis, K., and Frederick, W. *Business and Society.* 5th ed. New York: McGraw-Hill, 1984.

Demos, R. "Business and the Good Society." *Harvard Business Review* 33 (1955): 33–44.

Dierkes, M. "Social Performance in German Industry." Paper presented at the 38th Annual Meeting of the Academy of Management, San Francisco, 1978.

______. "A European Perspective on Business and Public Policy." Paper presented at the 42d Annual Meeting of the Academy of Management, New York, 1982.

Dierkes, M., and Antal, A. B. "Institutionalizing Corporate Social Responsiveness: Lessons Learned from Eight Years of Experimentation." Paper presented at the 44th Annual Meeting of the Academy of Management, Boston, 1984.

Dill, W. R. *Running the American Corporation.* Englewood Cliffs, N.J.: Prentice-Hall, 1978.

Donaldson, T. *Corporations and Morality.* Englewood Cliffs, N.J.: Prentice-Hall, 1982.

Donaldson, T., and P. Werhane. *Ethical Issues in Business: A Philosophical Approach.* Englewood Cliffs, N.J.: Prentice-Hall, 1979.

Donham, W. "Some Recent Books on Business Ethics." *Harvard Business Review* 15 (1927): 245–50.

Drucker, P. F. *The Future of Industrial Man.* 1942. Reprint. New York: The New American Library, 1965.

______. *The Concept of the Corporation.* 1946. Reprint. New York: The New American Library, 1972.

______. *Managing in Turbulent Times.* New York: Harper & Row, 1980.

______. "What Is 'Business Ethics'?" *The Public Interest* 63 (1981): 18–36.

Duddy, E. A. "The Moral Implications of Business as a Profession." *The Journal of Business* 18 (1946): 63–73.

Eells, R., and C. Walton. *Conceptual Foundations of Business.* Homewood, Ill.: Richard D. Irwin, 1962.

Epstein, E. M. "Business Ethics, Corporate Social Responsibility and Corporate Social Responsiveness: Distinctions Without Difference . . . or . . . Ne'er the Twain Will Meet . . . and Does It Really Matter." Presidential address at the Social Issues in Management Division, Academy of Management, Boston, 1984.

Evans, W. A. *Management Ethics: An Intercultural Perspective.* Boston: Martinus Nijhoff Medical Publishers, 1981.

Frederick, W. C. "The Growing Concern Over Business Responsibility." *California Management Review* 2 (1960): 54–56.

______. "Business and Society Curriculum: Suggested Guidelines for Accreditation." *AACSB Bulletin* 13 (1977): 1–5.

______. "From CSR1 to CSR2: The Maturing of Business and Society Thought." Working paper #279. Graduate School of Business, University of Pittsburgh, 1978.

______. "Toward CSR3: Why Ethical Analysis Is Indispensable and Unavoidable in Corporate Affairs." *California Management Review* 28 (1986): 126–41, 152–53.

Freeman, R. E. *Strategic Management: A Stakeholder Approach.* Marshfield, Mass.: Pitman, 1984.

Friedman, M. *Capitalism and Freedom.* Chicago: University of Chicago Press, 1962.

______. "The Social Responsibility of Business Is to Increase Its Profits." *New York Times Magazine*, September 13, 1970, 122–26.

Fritzsche, D. J., and H. Becker. "A Comparison of the Ethical Behavior of American and German Managers." Paper presented at the 43d Annual Meeting of the Academy of Management, Dallas, 1983.

______. "Business Ethics: A Cross-Cultural Comparison of Managers' Attitudes." Paper presented at the 44th Annual Meeting of the Academy of Management, Boston, 1984.

Garrett, T. M. *Ethics in Business.* London: Sheed & Ward, 1963.

Garrett, T. M., R. C. Baumhart, T. M. Purcell, and P. Rotes. *Cases in Business Ethics.* New York: Appleton-Century-Crofts, 1968.

Goodpastor, K. W., and J. B. Matthews, Jr. "Can a Corporation Have a Conscience?" *Harvard Business Review* 60 (1982): 132–41.

Gordon, R. A., and J. E. Howell. *Higher Education for Business.* New York: Columbia University Press, 1959.

Governance Committee of the Social Issues in Management Division of the Academy of Management. *Business and Society Curriculum: A Position Paper.* Boston: Academy of Management, 1976.

Grosse, R., and G. Perritt. *International Business Curricula: A Global Study.* Academy of International Business, 1980.

Hanson, K. O. "Business Schools Make Room for Corporate Social Policy." *Business and Society Review* no. 6 (1973): 75–80.

______. "Ethics and Business: A Progress Report." *Stanford GSB* (1983): 10–14.

______. Review of business ethics texts. *California Management Review* 26 (1983): 162–69.

Hauerwas, S. *Vision and Virtue.* Chicago: Fides/Claretian, 1974.

______. *Truth and Tragedy.* Notre Dame, Ind.: Notre Dame Press, 1977.

______. *A Community of Character.* Notre Dame, Ind.: Notre Dame Press, 1981.

Henderson, V. E. "The Ethical Side of Enterprise." *Sloan Management Review* 23 (1982): 37.

Hodges, L. H. *The Business Conscience.* Englewood Cliffs, N.J.: Prentice-Hall, 1963.

Hoffman, M. W., and J. M. Moore. "Results of a Business Ethics Curriculum Survey Conducted by the Center for Business Ethics." *Journal of Business Ethics* 2 (1982): 81–83.

Hoover, J. D., R. M. Troub, C. J. Whitehead, and L. G. Flores. "Social Performance Goals in the Peruvian and Yugoslav Worker Participation System." Paper presented at the 38th Annual Meeting of the Academy of Management, San Francisco, 1978.

Horowitz, I. L. "Social Science and Public Policy." In *Foundations of Political Sociology*, edited by I. L. Horowitz, pp. 369–94. New York: Harper & Row, 1972.

Jain, H. C. "Labor Market Problems of the Disadvantaged Workers: An Analysis of Approaches." Paper presented at the 38th Annual Meeting of the Academy of Management, San Francisco, 1978.

Johnson, H. L. "Can the Businessman Apply Christianity?" *Harvard Business Review* 35 (1957): 68–76.

______. "An Exploration of Remedies for Bribery in Foreign Markets." Paper presented at the 41st Annual Meeting of the Academy of Management, San Diego, 1981.

______. "A Brief Discussion of Bribery in Foreign Markets." Paper presented at the 42d Annual Meeting of the Academy of Management, New York, 1982.

Jones, D. C. *A Bibliography of Business Ethics.* 2d ed. Charlottesville, Va.: University of Virginia Press, 1982.

Keim, G. D., and R. E. Meiners. "Corporate Social Responsibility: Private Means for Public Wants." *Policy Review* 5 (1978): 83.

King, M. L. "Public Policy and Technological Innovation in Swedish Banking." Paper presented at the 44th Annual Meeting of the Academy of Management, Boston, 1984.

Kohlberg, L. *Essays on Moral Development.* New York: Harper & Row, 1981.

Konrad, A. R. "Are Business Ethics Worth Studying?" *Business and Society Review* no. 27 (1978): 54–57.

Kuhn, J. W., and I. Berg. *Values in a Business Society: Issues and Analysis.* New York: Harcourt, Brace & World, 1968.

Lebacqz, K. *Professional Ethics.* Nashville, Tenn.: Abingdon Press, 1985.

Lenway, S. "The Politics of Protection, Expansion and Escape: International Collaboration and Business Power in U.S. Foreign Trade Policy." Paper presented at the 44th Annual Meeting of the Academy of Management, Boston, 1984.

Levitt, T. "The Dangers of Social Responsibility." *Harvard Business Review* 36 (1958): 41–50.

Lodge, G. C. *The New American Ideology.* New York: Alfred A. Knopf, 1975.

McCoy, C. S. *Management of Values: The Ethical Difference in Corporate Policy and Performance.* Marshfield, Mass.: Pitman, 1985.

McGuire, J. *Business and Society.* New York: McGraw-Hill, 1963.

McMahon, T.F. *Report on the Teaching of Socio-Ethical Issues in Collegiate Schools of Business/Public Administration.* Charlottesville, Va.: Center for the Study of Applied Ethics, University of Virginia, 1975.

MacMillan, K. "The U.K. and European Experience." Paper presented at the 38th Annual Meeting of the Academy of Management, San Francisco, 1978.

______. "A Re-examination of Relationships Between Business Self-Interest, Wealth Creation and Community Well-Being." Paper presented at the 44th Annual Meeting of the Academy of Management, Boston, 1984.

Marcus, S., and K. O. Walters. "Assault on Managerial Autonomy." *Harvard Business Review* 56 (1978): 561.

Meek, C. "European Co-Determination." Paper presented at the 44th Annual Meeting of the Academy of Management, Boston, 1984.

Moore, C. E. *Principia Ethica*. Cambridge, England: Cambridge University Press, 1903.

Murphy, T. A. "Business and Society." *AACSB Bulletin* 11 (1975): 21–25.

National Affiliation of Concerned Business Students. *Survey of Corporate Social Policy Courses in Graduate Business Schools*. Palo Alto, Calif.: Stanford University, 1974.

National Commission on Excellence in Education. *A Nation at Risk: The Imperative for Educational Reform*. Washington, D.C.: National Commission on Excellence in Education, U.S. Department of Education, 1983.

Nozick, R. *Anarchy, State, and Utopia*. New York: Basic Books, 1974.

Ohmann, O. A. "'Skyhooks' with Special Implications for Monday through Friday." *Harvard Business Review* 33 (1955): 33–41.

______. "Search for a Managerial Philosophy." *Harvard Business Review* 25 (1957): 41–51.

Okun, A. M. *Equality and Efficiency: The Big Tradeoff*. Washington, D.C.: The Brookings Institution, 1975.

Opinion Research Corporation. *Codes of Ethics in Corporations and Trade Associations and the Teaching of Ethics in Graduate Business Schools: A Survey Conducted for the Ethics Resource Center*. Princeton, N.J., 1979.

Pastin, M. "Business Ethics by the Book." *Business Horizons* 28 (1985): 2–6.

Paul, K. "Business Ethics Steamroll the Professors." *Business and Society Review* no. 39 (1981): 40–41.

______. "Business Environment/Public Policy Questions for the 1980's." *Business and Society* 20–21 (1981–82): 11–16.

Paul, K., and R. Barbato. "The Multinational Corporation in the Less Developed Country: The Economic Development Model Versus the North-South Model." *Academy of Management Review* 10 (1985): 8–14.

Peters, T. J., and R. H. Waterman, Jr. *In Search of Excellence*. New York: Warner Books, 1982.

Petit, T. A. *The Moral Crisis in Management*. New York: McGraw-Hill, 1967.

Pierson, F. C. *The Education of the American Businessman: A Study of University-College Programs in Business Administration*. New York: McGraw-Hill, 1959.

Powers, C. W., and D. Vogel. *Ethics in the Education of Business Managers*. Hastings-on-Hudson, N.Y.: The Hastings Center, 1980.

Preston, L. E. "Corporation and Society: The Search for a Paradigm." *Journal of Economic Literature* 13 (1975): 434–53.

______. "Teaching Materials in Business and Society." *California Management Review* 25 (1983): 158–73. (Addendum privately circulated, March 1984.)

______. *Social Issues and Public Policy in Business and Management: Retrospect and Prospect*. College Park, Md.: Center for Business and Public Policy, University of Maryland, 1986.

Preston, L. E., and J. E. Post. *Private Management and Public Policy.* Englewood Cliffs, N.J.: Prentice-Hall, 1975.

Purcell, T. "Do Courses in Business Ethics Pay Off?" *California Management Review* 19 (1972): 50–58.

Rawls, J. *A Theory of Justice.* Cambridge: Harvard University Press, 1971.

Rey, F. "Corporate and Public Policy in France." Paper presented at the 38th Annual Meeting of the Academy of Management, San Francisco, 1978.

Schein, E. "Coming to a New Awareness of Organizational Culture." *Sloan Management Review* 25 (1984): 3–14.

Schendel, D. C., and C. W. Hofer, eds. *Strategic Management: A New View of Business Policy and Planning.* Boston: Little, Brown, 1979.

Schmidt, W., and M. Tannenbaum. "How to Choose a Leadership Pattern." *Harvard Business Review* 36 (1958): 95–101.

Schroeder, H., B. Sexty, F. LeCasse, and J. Pasquero. "Current Issues in the Canadian Business Environment." Paper presented at the 42d Annual Meeting of the Academy of Management, New York, 1982.

Seidler, L. J., and L. L. Seidler. *Social Accounting, Theory, Issues, and Cases.* Los Angeles: Melville Publishing, 1975.

Sethi, S. P. *The Unstable Ground: Corporate Social Policy in a Dynamic Society.* Los Angeles: Melville Publishing, 1974.

______. "Dimensions of Corporate Social Responsibility." *California Management Review* 3 (1975): 58–64.

______. "Business Response to Social Conflict: A Comparative Analysis." Paper presented at the 37th Annual Meeting of the Academy of Management, Orlando, 1977.

______. *Up Against the Corporate Wall.* 4th ed. Englewood Cliffs, N.J.: Prentice-Hall, 1982.

______. "Developing Effective International Business Strategies in a Changing Global Environment." Paper presented at the Annual Meeting of the Academy of International Business, London Business School, London, November 21–23, 1986.

Sethi, S. P., J. Cunningham, and J. M. Miller. *Corporate Governance: Public Policy-Social Responsibility Committee of the Corporate Board: Growth and Accomplishment.* Dallas: Center for Research in Business and Social Policy, The University of Texas at Dallas, 1979.

Sethi, S. P., and J. E. Post. "Marketing of Infant Formula Food in Less Developed Countries: Some Public Consequences of Private Action." Paper presented at the 38th Annual Meeting of the Academy of Management, San Francisco, 1978.

Sharp, F. C., and P. G. Fox. *Business Ethics.* New York: Appleton-Century-Crofts, 1937.

Steiner, G. *Business and Society.* New York: Random House, 1971.

______. "The Social Responsibilities of Business." Paper presented at a conference on "The Changing Business Role in Modern Society," Graduate School of Management, UCLA, Los Angeles, Calif., July 29–August 9, 1973.

Steiner, G. A., and J. B. Miner. *Management Policy and Strategy*. New York: Macmillan, 1982.

Steiner, G., and J. Steiner. *Business, Government and Society*. 4th ed. New York: Random House, 1985.

Stevens, G. E. "The Congruence of Ethics Between Managers Past and Present: Clark's Study Revisited." Paper presented at the 43d Annual Meeting of the Academy of Management, Dallas, 1983.

Task Force on Business and International Education. "Business and International Education." Occasional paper #4. Washington, D.C.: Government/Academic Interface Committee, 1977.

Taeusch, C. F. *Policy and Ethics in Business*. New York: McGraw-Hill, 1931.

Thompson, A. A., and A. J. Strickland III. *Strategy Formulation and Implementation: Tasks of the General Manager*. Revised ed. Plano, Tex.: Business Publications, 1983.

Tombari, H. A. *Business and Society*. Hinsdale, Ill.: Dryden Press, 1984.

Velasquez, M. G. *Business Ethics: Concepts and Cases*. Englewood Cliffs, N.J.: Prentice-Hall, 1982.

______. "Why Corporations Are Not Morally Responsible for Anything They Do." *Business and Professional Ethics Journal* 2 (Spring 1983): 1–18.

Vogel, D. "Corporate Responsibility and the Market Ethos: A Comparison of Great Britain and the United States." Paper presented at the 42d Annual Meeting of the Academy of Management, New York, 1982.

______. "The Study of Social Issues in Management: A Critical Appraisal." *California Management Review* 28 (1986): 142–51, 153–55.

Volard, S. V. "Developments in Industrial Democracy in Australia." Paper presented at the 43d Annual Meeting of the Academy of Management, Dallas, 1983.

Votaw, D. "History of Business and Public Policy Field." Working paper, 1986.

Votaw, D., and S. P. Sethi. "Do We Need a New Corporate Response to a Changing Social Environment?" Parts I and II. *California Management Review* 12 (1969): 3–16, 17–31.

______. *The Corporate Dilemma: Traditional Values verusus Contemporary Problems*. Englewood Cliffs, N.J.: Prentice-Hall, 1973.

Walters, K. D. "Who Should Control the Nationalized Company?" Paper presented at the 42d Annual Meeting of the Academy of Management, New York, 1982.

Walton, C., and R. Eeells. *The Business System*. New York: Macmillan, 1967.

Wartick, S. "The Special Challenge of Teaching Business and Society." Working paper #6, Kelce School of Business and Economics, Pittsburgh State University, 1982.

Wartick, S., and P. Cochran. "The Evolution of the Corporate Social Performance Model." *Academy of Management Review* 10 (1985): 758–69.

Weidenbaum, M. L. *The Future of Business Regulation.* New York: AMACOM, 1979.

_____ . *Business, Government, and the Public.* Englewood Cliffs, N.J.: Prentice-Hall, 1981.

Weidenbaum, J. L., and R. DeFina. *The Cost of Federal Regulation of Economic Activity.* Washington, D.C.: American Enterprise Institute, 1978.

Werhane, P. *Persons, Rights and Corporations.* Englewood Cliffs, N.J.: Prentice-Hall, 1985.

Wheelen, T. L., and D. Hunger. *Strategic Management.* Reading, Mass.: Addison-Wesley, 1984.

Williams, O. "Business Ethics: A Trojan Horse?" *California Management Review* 25 (1982): 14–24.

Wood, D. "Issues Briefs: Understanding the Business Environment." *Exchange* 6 (1981): 43–47.

Index

About the Editor

Karen Paul is associate professor of management at Rochester Institute of Technology. She has authored one previous book as well as many chapters and articles appearing in journals such as the *Academy of Management Review, Business and Society Review*, and *Business and Society*. Her current research concerns multinational corporations in South Africa, divestment and disinvestment, and the ethical investing movement. She is the 1987–88 Peace Fellow at the Mary Ingraham Bunting Institute of Radcliffe College.

About the Contributors

Otis W. Baskin is professor of management and director of the Center for Advanced Management Programs at the University of Houston-Clear Lake. He has authored six books and over thirty articles, and has been chairman of the Organizational Communication Division of the Academy of Management. His current research concerns the management of advanced technology organizations and the influence of external factors on managerial decision processes.

Otto A. Bremer is assistant to the president of Vesper Society and director of the Advanced Management Program of the Graduate Theological Union in Berkeley, California. He has published in the *Harvard Business Review, The Forum* of the Association for Social Economics, and numerous church and theological journals. He has worked in the area of ethics and values in management with particular research relating to religion and corporate management.

Rogene A. Buchholz is professor of business and public policy at the University of Texas at Dallas. He is the author or co-author of six books in the areas of business and public policy and business ethics. His articles have appeared in such journals as *Human Relations*, the *Journal of Management Studies, Personnel Psychology, Journal of Applied Psychology, Industrial and Labor Relations Review, Academy of Management Journal, Harvard Business Review*, and *Journal* *of Business Ethics.* His current research concerns the political strategies of corporations and ethical issues in business.

Philip L. Cochran is associate professor of business administration and director of the Center for Issues Management Research at The Pennsylvania State University. His articles have appeared in the *Academy of Management Journal, Academy of Management Review, California Management Review, Management International Review, Quarterly Journal of Business and Economics*, and other journals. His current research is in the areas of business ethics, corporate governance, corporate crime, and issues management.

David J. Fritszche is professor of business administration at the University of Portland. He has published two books, as well as numerous articles in journals including the *Academy of Management Journal, Journal of Marketing Research, Journal of Consumer Affairs, Journal of Business Ethics*, and *Journal of the Academy of Marketing Science.* His current research is in the area of marketing ethics.

Gerald Keim is a professor of management at Texas A&M University. He has published in many journals, including the *Academy of Management Review*, the *Academy of Management Journal, Policy Review, Public Choice, Journal of Politics, Sloan Managemet Review,* and *California Management Review.* He consults widely, participates in the Washington Campus executive program in Washington, D.C., and has been a visiting professor at Stanford University. His research focuses on the interface between corporations and their external environment, especially corporate political activity.

John E. Logan is associate professor of management at the University of South Carolina. He is the author of several monographs, articles, and cases, and has published in journals such as the *Journal of Risk and Insurance* and the *American Journal of Small Business.* His current research interests are in the area of social issues in management, with particular emphasis on entrepreneurship and innovation.

John Mahon is associate professor of management policy at Boston University. He has won numerous awards, both locally and nationally, for teaching. His articles have appeared in journals which include the *Strategic Management Journal, Journal of Long Range*

Planning, Academy of Management Review, California Management Review, Journal of Contemporary Business, Journal of Small Business Management, and the annual volume, *Research in Corporate Social Performance and Policy*. His current research is on corporate political strategies, the impact of regulation and deregulation, and issues in stakeholder management.

George C. Sawyer is a professor in the Economics Department of City College of New York, and also president of Management Technology & Resources, consultants in business growth, planning, and corporate strategy. He has also been director of corporate planning and director of commercial technology management for Hoffman-La Roche. He is senior editor of *Planning Review* and monograph editor for The Planning Forum. He has published six books and numerous articles. His current research interests are in the areas of venture analysis, commercial development, and acquisition processes.

Steven L. Wartick is assistant professor of business administration and a faculty associate of the Center for Issues Management Research at The Pennsylvania State University. His publications include articles in journals such as the *Academy of Management Review, California Management Review*, and *Business Horizons*. His current research interests are in the areas of corporate social performance, issues management, and business-government relations.

Richard E. Wokutch is associate professor of management at Virginia Polytechnic Institute and State University. He has published articles in journals such as the *California Management Review, Journal of Public Policy and Marketing, Journal of Accounting and Public Policy*, and *Journal of Business Ethics*, as well as in the annual volume, *Research in Corporate Social Performance and Policy*. His current research is in the areas of business ethics, social auditing, ethical investing, and the management of occupational safety and health in multinational business.